From Mummy

With Love

A GIFT OF MULTILINGUAL PARENTING

Tra My Nguyen, PhD

To my baby Mỡ,

from mummy

with love.

CONTENTS

PREFACE

Having had a lot of things to write about, like many people, I never did. But recently, I had an unexplainable urge to write, and a book poured out of my head onto paper in what felt like a single second. Once all the raw thoughts were written down, I started a two-year-long process of moulding them, crafting them, and making sure I would want to read them if I were not myself. There is no time like the present, so here it goes.

All of the things included in this book come from my heart, my own life experiences, and motherhood. You can be sure that the advice given is based on many hours of careful, thorough, and fact-based research. As my day job, I am a university lecturer and an academic researcher, so I understand the importance of credibility, reliability, and relevance of any statements, conclusions, suggestions, and recommendations that are released into the world. Even more importantly, I know that most of my readers are parents, and that the health and development of our children is our top priority. For this reason, this book comes from the most sacred place in my heart, which is being a mother.

I am not one to tell you about having balance in your life—juggling work, kids, home, family, and every other unnamed thing that you have to do—because, well, I have no clue about it. Before tying the knot, I was a workaholic. And even before that, I was a studyholic. The day I got a positive pregnancy test, I became obsessed with all things pregnancy. Imagine waking up frantically thinking about one thing, scouring the Internet, bookstores, and libraries for information about it, and continuing to think about it frantically until the night falls; that was me and pregnancy—a little too obsessive to be completely honest.

Then, the birth of my son marked the day
I became consumed by motherhood.

I still work because I like having a career, and self-actualization is important to me. But really, the biggest priority in my life has since shifted to my son, his development, his emotional wellbeing, and his happiness.

This by no means implies that I am a perfect mother.
I am probably the most flawed mother of all.

But I am the perfect mother for my son because he is a part of me, and I am a part of him. We're two but one, and that's all that matters.

This book was written in chunks over many nights as the dark sky fell upon the city of Hanoi (Vietnam) and my son was fast asleep. He would usually sleep soundly for a few hours before he stirred and required attention around 3 in the morning. I would use those few hours to jot down rough paragraphs before tending to him.

The idea for this book sparked as I began my journey into motherhood. I am trilingual, and my upbringing was in a multilingual environment. To be more precise, I grew up in Poland and went to Polish schools where Polish was the main language and English was taught as a foreign language. My family was Vietnamese and always used Vietnamese as the only language at home. Whenever at school or out in public, the language used for all communications was Polish.

Then, I started an International Baccalaureate (IB) high school program where classes were conducted entirely in English, but my peers and teachers were still Polish, so school time itself was a bilingual environment, while the language I used at home with my family remained strictly Vietnamese. This multilingual upbringing cultivated a strong linguistic foundation in me, as I found that my ability to learn and absorb new languages as well as adapt to new circumstances and new situations was, not to boast or anything, relatively impressive.

Later in life, I found myself highly adaptable to new people, surroundings, and environments.

For my toddler son though, the situation is not quite the same. His environment is not multilingual by default. He was born in Vietnam, is being raised in Vietnam, and goes to preschool with Vietnamese children. The geographical situation of my son's upbringing does not naturally provide opportunities for multilingualism.

Having less than perfectly aligned circumstances, however, does not justify settling for less.

Even before I became pregnant, I was determined

that I would not let my linguistic privilege go to waste. I made a decision that I would not allow my child to struggle with learning English at school like most other children I see around me.

So I gave in to my obsession and did a lot of research on how to raise children who speak two languages. I made a plan for how to create the most suitable environment to raise my child as (at least) bilingual, even though my husband speaks only Vietnamese. Neither do my parents nor any other member of the extended family, except my brother.

Besides English, I am also fluent in Polish, as I grew up and studied there, but I do not intend to teach my son Polish. Realistically, Polish is not as useful a language as English, and I mean that with utmost respect.

I want my son to be natively fluent in both Vietnamese and English. The key word is "natively fluent" rather than just "fluent." I want him to naturally command both languages rather than have one as his mother tongue and the other as a foreign language. The only way to do that, I figured, was to cultivate both languages simultaneously from the very start. And I was the only one to do it, as I was the only one who spoke English well enough in the entire family.

If you are like some parents out there and all you care about is your child's weight gain, then you will naturally focus on *nutrition*. Your child will be extremely well-fed, maybe in the high percentile for their weight and height, but regretfully, their brain will not receive as much stimulation as it would have if you focused equally as much on their *play*. And I am a firm believer that you can always put on extra weight later on if needed, but you can't always stretch your brain. This is not to say that nutrition is not important, because it is. Nutrition is extremely important but not *time-sensitive* - brain development is. Whatever you focus all your energy on, that thing will thrive. Some parents choose weight gain, while some choose brain stimulation.

I would like to share a quote from my personal journal with the hope that it will shed some light on the type of mother and person that I am. Then you can decide for yourself if I am trustworthy enough for you to invest your precious time in reading the rest of this book. The following excerpt is from an entry on the 21st of November 2021, poured directly from my soul onto paper exactly at midnight:

"*I'm thinking about motherhood. Well, I always think about motherhood. But today, as I refrained myself from losing patience with my 2-year-old toddler, I thought about how people choose to have children, then go on to complain about how hard it is. Yes, it is hard, but I wouldn't have it any other way. I don't think I've ever loved anything or anyone more than my son. And even thinking about the possibility of him getting hurt literally turns my gut upside down. I look at the stairs and imagine what if my son fell down the stairs, and my stomach instantly feels as if it's twisted. I look at scissors and randomly imagine what if my son gets a cut no matter how small, and I instantly get light-headed. They keep telling you that you won't feel your parents' love until you have kids of your own. But, and I say this with all the respect in the world, I don't think there are parents on this planet that love their kids more than I love my son (which I know is not true, but sometimes I feel that way regardless). My dearest son is without a doubt a handful, to say the least. Not many people will believe that at 25 months old, he still doesn't sleep through the night. They would criticize me, criticize my parenting, criticize my son, criticize his growth, and eventually criticize everything else in my life. But when the night falls, it's just us three - you, me and your daddy - and nobody else. It is our cocoon, our life, our story. Your daddy's and my parenthood is our own sacred experience. And it will be as it has to be. Or rather, as it is meant to be."*

This book not only fulfils my lifelong dream of being a published author, but it is also a truthful and personal collection of my experiences and insights. I share my multilingualism knowledge, reiterate, and emphasize the benefits and importance of multilingualism or bilingualism for our children if introduced and implemented properly from an early age.

I worked on this book for over two years, and I hope that I have included all that I know on the topic of multilingual parenting. If it turns out that I end up knowing more and have more to say on this matter (which I expect and hope that I will), then there will be a continuation of the book in the form of a revised edition or a new volume altogether. For now, let's dive into my brain and soul in all their glory.

THE SCIENCE BEHIND
MULTILINGUALISM

Before we dive in, let's count through the definitions first to make sure we are on the same page, as many of the books I have read about multilingualism tend to mix up the interpretation of the common terms. According to the Cambridge dictionary, *multilingualism* is defined as "the ability to use more than two languages for communication, whether written or spoken". It is different from *monolingualism*, which is "the ability to use one language well". *Trilingualism* refers to "the ability to use three languages well", and *bilingualism* refers to "the ability to use two languages well", both of which are forms of multilingualism. In this book, we will talk about all forms of multilingualism. Sometimes, I use the terms "multilingual" and "bilingual" interchangeably. If you are like me and you have successfully instilled the love of a second language in your child, at some point before your child turns six, your mind will start to wander and you will strategically plan to introduce another language to the mix, giving your child the most precious gift of life, besides unconditional love, which is a world of opportunity.

Since the 1990s were named the "Decade of the Brain" by a presidential resolution, a lot of research has been done on the brains of bilingual children and how being bilingual or multilingual affects cognitive development. Researchers have found that the brains of children who speak more than one language work differently than the brains of children who only speak one language. The largest chunk of brain development takes place in the first six years of a child's life.

It is a well-known fact that the first six years of a child's life are the best and most important time for them to learn how to think, focus, speak, and even develop some personality traits. The brain of a child grows and changes the most between birth and age six. The extent to which the brain is stimulated during these early years has a long-term effect on a child's ability to learn and perform well in school and in life. Hence, the quality of a child's first few years of life, both positive and negative, considerably affects how their brain develops. At birth, the brain of an average baby is about a quarter the size of the brain of an average adult. It grows twice as big in the first year, which is amazing. It keeps getting bigger until it's about eighty percent of its adult size at age three and ninety percent of its adult size at age six.

Many studies of preschool-aged children from different countries have found that bilinguals' general cognitive abilities improve regardless of the number of languages they know or how close or far apart the languages are typologically (be it Vietnamese and English or Greek, Korean, and French). There is a substantial difference in brain development between monolinguals and bilinguals, though. The brain is a part of the body that runs everything. When a baby is born, they have all of the brain cells (neurons) they'll ever have, but it's the connections between these cells that make the brain work. It is noteworthy that the first six years are the period when a child spends most of their time at home with their family. This means that most of a child's brain development takes place long before he or she starts elementary school. When we (parents) delay the learning of English (the non-mother tongue) until primary school, it is already too late to learn English effortlessly. Are you one of those people who took foreign language classes for three years in high school but still can't even ask for directions or have a meaningful conversation in the language? When a child learns a language at a young age, it gives them a huge cognitive and linguistic head start. It will also help them "breeze" through foreign language classes in high school and college, giving them a chance to become truly bilingual and even enjoy it. A missed golden period (the first six years) creates an unnecessary need for a child to struggle and learn the non-mother language consciously rather than subconsciously as they would have done during the first six years.

Your child's brain is like a sponge. It has the ability to absorb without limits. It is truly miraculous and incredible what a child actually learns in the first six years of life—not just language but also skills, habits, actions, personality, temperament, how to react to and what to say in different situations. Everything that makes life possible, a child can learn from a very young age. I get a lot of comments along the lines of, "Your child can't even speak the mother tongue properly yet; why would you even bother teaching a foreign language?" "Your child will just end up confused and unable to properly communicate in any of the languages." *I beg to differ.* Even before I had kids, I strongly believed this to be untrue simply based on my own personal experience and my own upbringing. Luckily, science backs me up. I have done my research on early childhood development. So, to answer the first question that might be hovering in your mind right now:

No, bilingualism will not create confusion between the languages, and your child will not end up impaired in any of the languages.

Multilingual people subconsciously develop very complex executive functions of the brain. These refer to the functions of the prefrontal cortex, a region of the brain that is responsible for the regulation and control of adaptive and goal-directed behavior. When a monolingual hears a word, all they have to do is compare it with their own personal language rule set for how that phoneme (sound) relates to a particular meaning. However, those who speak more than one language have the added complexity of maintaining multiple language rule sets in their brains. If a Spanish-Italian bilingual hears the phonemes *b-u-r-r-o*, using their multiple language stocks, which are stored separate from each other, they will know that the speaker meant either "donkey" in Spanish or "butter" in Italian.

I get plenty of comments from other parents, with the general message being "Babies should be babies; forcing them to learn languages at such a young age is unnecessary as they will learn it at school anyway." With all due respect, it's easy to see that the first few years of a child's life are when they learn languages the fastest and easiest. Young children learn things that interest them. They never struggle or suffer when learning something. Quite the contrary, their eyes sparkle when they learn something new. So why would we want our children to have to sit through endless hours of boring language classes when they can absorb it through play long before they even start school? How often do we encounter children who are better-spoken than their peers? Is it because they're inherently better, or perhaps it's because they got more frequent and higher-quality language exposure when they were little? Children don't just repeat what their parents say, they also copy the way their parents speak. In addition to their parents, who are their main role models, children also pick up language from other places. Therefore, the people, the environment, and the kinds of languages that your child is exposed to during the first few years of life are of extreme importance in shaping who they become and how developed their language gets. All these factors combined essentially create a combination of "language ingredients", which, teamed up with their own persona, eventually yield their own unique version of navigating a certain language.

Language absorption begins even before birth. Evidence-based research has shown that fetuses in the womb, at different stages of pregnancy, begin to feel, hear, and even see. Through changes of movement, sound, and light, babies' earliest experience of communication begins when they are still in their mother's "cocoon". The environment outside of the mother's womb is highly dynamic, but babies can recognize familiar sounds and movements. As soon as babies are born, despite meeting their father for the first time, they can recognize him, or rather his voice, assuming the father was frequently present when the baby was inside the mother's womb. Even as early as 1984, behavioral scientist Kolata G. used tested methods to show that fetuses can and do learn [1]. In the modern era, more and more research is being done on education and learning before birth, and there is a lot of focus on trying out prenatal education by giving pre-birth interventions to babies while they are still in the womb. According to Dr. Shelina Bhamani of Aga Khan University [2], babies in the womb learn through experiences, repetition, and association. Babies hear familiar voices and music in the womb and are comforted by them after birth. The gentle rocking motion of a car may be soothing to a baby because it mimics the feel of a mother's womb. If a mother talks to the baby in the womb over and over again, the baby may respond right away. The baby may associate what you say with how you feel. If you're sad and talk to your baby in the womb, those words will also be sad, or feel sad. Similar patterns apply to other emotions, such as happiness, excitement, anger, frustration, among others.

It makes sense to think that language development begins during pregnancy, but the most sensitive language development period is believed to be from three to six years of age. This is when the child can, for the most part, in their own unique ways, express themselves. Their language formation consists of both verbal and bodily "ingredients," whatever it takes to convey their messages. During this golden period, children are also extremely observant of the way that parents and other people around them communicate. They are not afraid of expressing their thoughts and ideas, and they self-correct almost instantly given the right motivation and guidance. All these little "ingredients" collected throughout their early years help form their own perception of the world as well as their communication abilities and relationships later in life.

Human interaction is key
in childhood language development.

More often than necessary, we see children who watch TV and cartoons all day long. Even though the TV characters talk and sing the whole time, in reality, these children tend to have delayed language development. The key is in the lack of human interaction to model speech and language for them. I have made it my life's mission to educate myself to the best of my abilities as an academic and researcher on childhood education and development so that I can give my son the best possible environment and opportunities to become the best version of himself. Opposing a considerable amount of advice given by people around me who undoubtedly love my son, I made a conscious decision not to leave my son's educational future to chance.

I found that the most effective way to nurture your child's early communication skills is by creating the right linguistic environment. If you are a parent who is raising your child to be bilingual and if you are multilingual yourself, then at one point or another in your life, you will have encountered a person who will say something along the lines of: "Don't teach the kids more than one language at a time because you will end up confusing them," or "Your child will not be able to use any of the languages properly." Well, with all due unsarcastic respect, to those people, I have got nothing to say. I would like to, however, reiterate the top five benefits of bilingualism. This is by no means an exhaustive list. Raising your child in a bilingual environment bears numerous advantages. These include higher intelligence compared to those who are monolingual; higher creativity, higher cognitive abilities, better communication skills, and last, but impossible to omit from this list, greater social skills, which lead on to creating better life opportunities for your child in the near and far future. Having said that, obviously, if you provide your child with bilingualism in a careless and thoughtless way, then you might be doing more harm than good. So, this section of the book is dedicated to creating a carefully thought out and appropriate environment for your child to develop their language skills in one, two, three, or even more languages. And I would like to extend this beyond just language development and include the aspect of developing communication skills in general.

What we need to understand is that children come into the world as a blank piece of paper. They learn everything from the environment around them. Their communication skills and language skills will essentially come from the exposure to language and communication that they are given. It is unreasonable to expect that your child will automatically know how to communicate with different types of people, in different scenarios, and how to react to different situations if you fail to give them appropriate guidance. The critical time to start seriously applying this principle is around eighteen months of age, when the child is starting to speak. Some children might start to talk much earlier, and some children might start to talk much later, but I give eighteen months as an average for the start of *spoken language development*. Of course, communication doesn't mean merely *talking*; your child has actually been communicating with you for a very long time before they vocalized their first word. Communication begins as early as in your womb where fetuses communicate through movements (like kicking). Early communication skills after birth, such as calling for attention and expressing emotions through cries and cues, body language, little smirks and smiles, and laughter are babies' ways of communicating with their parents. Children who are exposed to two languages from birth usually start making their first sounds and words at the same age as children who are only exposed to one language. Also, the pattern of vocabulary and grammatical growth for bilingual children is very similar to that of children who only speak one language. The kinds of words children learn and the relationship between vocabulary and grammatical growth in each language follow the same pattern as for children who only speak one language [3, 4].

Still, the effect of bilingualism on the ability to speak and understand a language is often described as a "delay" in learning vocabulary and grammar. Some studies have shown that, on average, bilingual children reach basic vocabulary and grammatical milestones at the same age as monolingual children. However, other studies have shown that bilinguals have a smaller vocabulary in each language than monolinguals and are behind on grammatical tests when skills are measured in a single language [5]. Since a lot of research has shown that children's language skills depend on how much language they hear, these results don't come as a surprise. People who speak more than one language divide their time between the two, so they hear less of each language on average. Importantly, though, studies show over and over that when both languages are taken into account, bilingual children do not fall behind their monolingual peers. For example, when a child's vocabulary in both languages is added together, it is the same as or larger than that of a child who only speaks one language. There are similar results from tests of grammar knowledge [6]. As with children who only speak one language, the rate of vocabulary and grammar growth in bilingual children is related to how much and how well they hear speech in each language [7, 8]. In line with these findings, the way the brains of bilingual children react to words in each language depends on how much they know about each language. In particular, the more dominant language of bilingual children has more mature brain activation patterns than the less dominant language [9].

Once children start to verbally communicate, parents' job is to give them the proper ways of describing things, naming emotions, and retelling events. What I mean is that you "hand" them the vocabulary to communicate verbally in each situation. If you don't consciously do this, they will eventually learn, but they will be forced to learn through bits and pieces that they pick up from everyday life. They might learn things that you don't want them to learn, such as curse words, slang, and age-inappropriate language. Some adults may find it "funny" when a child commands age-inappropriate language, but the more sensible parents (the ones reading this book) will realize the *Iceberg Effect*, where ninety percent of the impact is not immediately visible. The language and communication development of children navigates the development of their whole-being. Poor communication development largely hinders other aspects of their cognitive development.

A better and faster approach to enhancing your child's communication development is to give them the vocabulary and communication techniques that they can just use instantly. You may ask what I mean by "give them the vocabulary". "My child is only a year and a half", "How do I give them ready-to-use vocabulary?" An illustration of this is simple. For example, you and your child go for a walk, and your child seems to be looking at a moving bus on the street. Being mindfully present allows you to observe your child and notice that they are looking at something specific, which will prompt you to say the name of that thing or describe the observation. You can say: "That's a blue bus, isn't it?" This principle especially applies to your child's feelings. The key is in your mindful, present observation and your understanding of your child's whole being. When you see that your child is happy, verbally name that emotion: "This is so much fun, isn't it?" or "Are you happy?" When your child looks sad, confirm that you acknowledge it by saying: "Are you sad?" If your child gives you a response such as a nod, you can expand on the topic by asking: "Why are you sad?", "It's okay to feel sad," or "Do you want to sit next to mummy?".

Your primary goal should be to let your child feel that they are *heard, seen,* and *understood*. It is okay to let them feel what they feel. After all, they are indeed *little* humans, but their emotions are very *big*, and that's okay. As long as the situation is not dangerous and you can safely delay attending to the pain immediately, help your child navigate the situation by identifying their own emotions and gauging how they should respond: should they cry hysterically right away, or would it be okay to just tell mummy/daddy about what happened? This entire step takes less than a minute. Use simple, direct, age-appropriate language to help your child identify what they are feeling, be it shock, pain, or sadness.

Gradually, your child will start to tell you how they feel and how they deal with it instead of you having to resolve hysteria every time. These mini experiences strengthen the bond between the child and the parent because the child feels that they are always seen, heard, and understood. When your child trusts you completely, there is an enormous power in parenting. As time goes by, your child starts to develop a more diverse vocabulary and is able to command language in a more versatile manner. You need to continue your role as their first and most important teacher. You must ensure that your child knows you understand them. Instead of just nodding, brushing it off, or simply responding "really?", "wow", or "yeah?", show them that you really understand what they are communicating with you by repeating what they said. You would be amazed at the difference in their mental state once they are certain they are understood. They feel encouraged to tell you even more just because they know you understand.

Young children, however, often don't speak very clearly, and sometimes Mum is the only person who can fully understand their speech, but if Mum doesn't pay enough attention, even she might not be able to "translate" every word. If this happens, try to avoid saying, "I don't understand what you are saying", because gradually it will seep into your child's mind and turn into frustration. In their communication with you, everything is clear to them. If they sense that they can't be understood by *you*, then a bigger question might pop up in their little heads: "Then *who*?". You are supposedly the person who understands them the most in the whole wide world. So, you need to step up and own that role. To some parents, this comes very naturally. To others, they might have to make a bit more of an effort.

To make sure that your child is understood by other people in larger gatherings, you might want to encourage your child to keep communicating by repeating what he/she says so that it is clear to others. That way, others can understand your child and your child feels he/she is understood (communication proves effective). However, this might not always be possible as it would be physically supernatural to hover above their heads and constantly repeat what they're saying to everyone, everywhere. You can be your own judge as to when your "assistance" is needed and your repetition of your child's words to their friend or the friend's parent is beneficial. Generally, your goal is to make your child feel as if he is fully understood and his communication efforts do not go to waste. That way, he will be encouraged to communicate even more and more each day.

You will see a significant improvement on a daily

basis, even from morning to afternoon, because toddlers learn extremely quickly. If your toddler conveys a message to you that you understand but is incorrectly articulated, repeat that same message to them in the "correct" way while trying to use as much of your child's original wording as possible. Your child will instantly understand that saying it your way will help him/her be understood better. The change (or "self-correction") will happen effortlessly without you having to explain to him what the right and wrong way is. Your child's communication skills will just evolve on their own as long as you, the parent, are mindful and respectful.

Another aspect, and very often an obstacle, in communication development in very young children is the ability to *process their own emotions*. It is no secret that young children often have meltdowns, commonly referred to as tantrums, especially around the age two to four. As hard as it might be to believe for some parents, your child is not misbehaving on purpose nor deliberately trying to cause you trouble and inconvenience. Shining through their little tiny bodies are paramount impulsive emotions and a very limited ability to deal with the emotional outbursts. Our job is to see through that instead of just focusing on the misbehaving outer shell. We, as parents, must see through the shell and realize the smallness of our children. We must realize that their emotions are bigger than they are. Not only will that help your child learn to feel accepted, but it will also help you feel more empathy for your child instead of sheer exasperation. Breaking through the tantrum-shell will help you be a more understanding parent, help your child trust you more, and learn to process their own emotions. As adults, they will be able to control their own emotions instead of having sudden, impulsive, uncontrollable outbursts. Our own quality of life is essentially determined by how we deal with what is thrown at us, which largely consists of thousands of various situations and resulting emotions. Just like in our own experience, sometimes it is enough to just sit by your child in silence and wait for the emotion to pass. After that, you can carry on or briefly touch upon the incident by saying: "You felt sad, huh?" or "I completely understand." Gradually, these little incidents and how they are dealt with will build into your child's subconsciousness that their emotions are valid and it is okay to feel what they feel. They will learn that feeling all those things is quite normal, and they will gradually learn how to cope with and control those big emotions.

Similarly, when they do something wrong or communicate with you in the "wrong" way, such as hitting, shouting, hurting, using inappropriate language, do not immediately criticize. Instead, repeat their message in the correct and appropriate way, then just let the negativity slide by. It might seem like you're not doing much, perhaps it might feel like you should discipline or punish them for misbehaving. However, letting it pass by not reacting is very often a more effective response. If you dwell on the negative aspect of your child's communication, this is all they are going to remember, see, and focus on. You don't want that. You want them to feel confident, happy, and positive about their communication skills. If you don't approve of something, instead of nagging and criticizing that one particular thing, it is a more effective strategy to simply let it go. Don't react. Bad behavior thrives on reactions. Particularly when it comes to bad language, just let it go. Don't repeat it, don't react, and your child will just forget about it. Very often, we witness situations where a child uses inappropriate language that they have picked up from somewhere/someone. As soon as the child says it, the whole family reacts, either surprised, upset, or even amused. Maybe the bad word sounds "funny" coming from a three-year-old's mouth, but is it actually funny if your child learns to use that language consistently and frequently? You've got to think about that.

Parenting is a long-haul project
without a chance to scrap-and-redo.

Thoughtless language often occurs during car trips, where poor driving happens on the road, which frustrates us, so we call that poor driver names. Meanwhile, your child is right there in the back seat "absorbing" all that language, and maybe later that day, maybe the next week, or the next month, your child will use that language in a random situation. Maybe it fits that particular situation, maybe it doesn't, but again, adults might find it surprising, upsetting, or (sadly) amusing. If you don't want your child to make a habit of using bad language, then the most effective way is just to let it slide. Do not react. If your child's behavior or language doesn't get a reaction, then in your child's mind, it's not worth repeating, it's not fun, it's not interesting. Consequently, your child will simply stop using it and quickly forget about it.

When your child says something incorrectly, how do you respond? Inappropriate language issues aside, imagine that they are trying to tell you something, but they pronounce a word or phrase incorrectly, especially in a foreign language. How do you correct them? For example, my son started off at twenty-two-month-old with some very "difficult" English words, such as "bridge". This word is not the easiest to pronounce but my son was interested in bridges, roads, buildings, and trees - infrastructure seemed to interest him. He really liked the word "bridge", and I took this opportunity to embrace his interest and teach him the word "bridge". At first, he couldn't pronounce it correctly, obviously. I didn't repeat his "baby pronunciation" but rather pronounced it correctly instead. I applauded him for saying this word (even though incoherently) every single time, showing that I understood and appreciated what he was saying. I repeated the word "bridge" (in the correct pronunciation) every time he said it over and over again. For a couple of months, his pronunciation kept evolving every single day. I could hear a difference in the way that he pronounced the word "bridge", from what was completely inaudible to an almost perfect pronunciation of that word at just two years of age.

This mindful approach also applies to situations where you ask your child a question and they give you a (factually) wrong answer. For example, imagine you ask your child to name the color of something that is blue, but your child says red. Do you simply say they are wrong? You could. Many parents do. But a better way, which will help your child learn something without sacrificing his self-confidence is to say "oh red? that is red" and point to an object nearby that is red. Then point to the initial object and say, "this is blue". This subtle method helps correct your child's (factually) wrong answer without making them feel discouraged. If you tell your child that they are wrong often enough, then your child will actually start feeling like a failure, because every answer they give seems to be wrong. Instead of pointing out directly that your child is wrong, simply redirect their attention to make their answer somewhat correct, and then follow up by giving them the correct answer to the initial question. I found it extremely effective for learning colors, shapes, names of animals, learning vocabulary, and numbers. At just two and a half years old, my son seemed to be able to correct his own mistakes very quickly while still feeling like he's doing a great job.

Multilingualism is not a newly discovered concept; it's been around for centuries. So I wondered what the *commonly known strategies for raising multilingual children* were. Initial research on raising bilingual children, which can be conducted by anyone through a simple strategy called "google it" pops up a few common notions. They are commonly known as the three most effective strategies to raise bilingual children: "one parent, one language," "minority language at home," and "time and place strategy". I will explain each strategy, and in the chapters that follow, *I will explain to you why these strategies will not work*. Depending on the particular dynamics of your family, where you live, and where you are raising your child or children, one or more of these methods might work for you. You might even want to adopt these strategies but also modify them to arrive at the version that works best for you and your family. A language strategy can be chosen for both practical and emotional reasons. Some parents choose a language strategy without making a conscious or well-thought-out choice. Instead, they do it naturally, based on things like how they talk as a couple, how well they speak another language, or just their instincts and wants. Others, on the other hand, are very aware of how they need to speak both languages to their children to help them become bilingual. This must be a conscious choice which requires a lot of persistence from the parents. We must decide how to give our children both quality and quantity of language exposure, mostly through social interaction, based on their own language skills and preferences, as well as the situation in the community where they live.

One Parent, One Language

A core premise of this strategy is that each parent would speak a different language with the children, and they would learn both languages simultaneously without any confused sense of identity. The most common scenario is that the parents each come from a different country speaking a different mother tongue. Parents may opt for this strategy because they value the emotional connection that comes with speaking the *minority language* (meaning lesser used, or heritage language) to their child. They wish to instill in their child a sense of cultural pride and heritage, or see it as an investment in the child's future academic and professional success. "One parent, one language" strategy works well when you are trying to raise a trilingual child.

An example can be as follows: "you are Vietnamese, your spouse is American, and you all live in Poland. You want your child to speak Vietnamese, English, and Polish. Using the "one parent, one language" strategy, the key is that you speak to your child at all times in Vietnamese only, your spouse in English only, and you let the child learn Polish outside of the home when they are at school or hanging out with friends. It works great in a situation where each parent is natively fluent in a different language. It doesn't really work if both parents are of the same nationality and neither of them is really fluent in another language, because then it would create weirdness and inconvenience in daily communication.

Remember that passing on a language is not a one-afternoon exercise; it is something that you must commit to doing persistently throughout the many years of raising your child. Whatever language each parent chooses to speak to the child has to be the language that the parent is comfortable communicating in. Little daily phrases that burst out as a result of daily emotions usually occur in one's native language rather than a learned one. It can't be a forced thing, because then daily communication with your child would just come out unnatural and, at the cost of bonding, defeat the purpose of establishing bilingualism in your child.

Minority Language at Home

This strategy actually works when both parents are

of the same nationality but live in a different country. For example, both mum and dad are Vietnamese but the family lives in Poland. According to this strategy, both parents would strictly speak Vietnamese (the minority language) at home to each other and to the child. The child will learn Polish (the majority language) outside of the home. In this situation, you are not required to actively teach your child Polish. You only need to make sure that the child is natively fluent in Vietnamese by speaking this language at home at all times with your child.

This was sort of the way I was raised. Although I am trilingual, I did learn two of my languages this way. My parents strictly spoke Vietnamese at home, and I learned Polish outside of the home. My parents were not fluent in Polish, so they didn't make any effort to teach me Polish as they knew they would teach it wrong. They knew I would learn proper Polish anyway because we lived in Poland, I went to Polish schools, and I had Polish friends. Instead, my parents made a special effort to make sure that I could speak Vietnamese fluently, effortlessly, and correctly by communicating strictly in Vietnamese at home. Even though it was easier for me and my brother to talk to each other in Polish at home, we weren't allowed to. Evidently, this strategy worked very well because, compared to my peers who grew up in a similar environment with Vietnamese parents living in Poland, my brother and I were able to command the Vietnamese language in a way that my peers did not. Moreover, they weren't able to properly read or write in Vietnamese despite having attended weekly Vietnamese language classes organized by Vietnamese people living in Poland (it was called "Lac Long Quan School"), which my brother and I did not attend. My peers essentially identified themselves as Polish citizens, which is probably one of the biggest traps, sometimes a sacrifice, of settling down in a foreign country. Many of my parents' friends, who were of Vietnamese origin and lived in Poland, spoke to their children in broken Polish, even at home. Not only was this hindering the children's opportunities to learn their mother tongue (Vietnamese), but it also damaged the correctness of their Polish.

One of the fruits of my parents' efforts and vision is that although I lived, studied, and worked entirely in

Europe for the first twenty five years of my life, when I returned to Vietnam, I still adapted quickly to the unique Vietnamese ways. I even worked at a public university and taught majors in both English and Vietnamese. It sure wasn't easy, but I did it.

Time and Place

This strategy resembles creating a habit for your child in terms of languages. This strategy is suitable for situations where both parents and other members of the family are at least bilingual. For example, everyone would speak the first language at mealtime, and everyone would speak the second language during playtime. The idea is that there is a designated time and place for each language to create an unconditional habit for the child to be able to use both languages in a natural environment. Although this strategy is likely to cultivate strong natural abilities to communicate in both languages, the drawback is perhaps impracticality and inconvenience. All members of the family must be in on this and be mindful about switching across languages. Depending on the level of strategy adaptation, one other drawback might be limited vocabulary as the child might be able to use a certain language in certain situations only, particularly those that resemble the time and place for that language. Oftentimes, life happens, and it's not always possible to be strictly consistent about using a certain language in a certain situation every single day. But it is okay.

It is not like if you fail to implement one strategy correctly, then your child's bilingualism is doomed. You do you - that is, what is best for you, your life, your family, your child.

COMMON MYTHS
ABOUT MULTILINGUALISM

Language Development Delay

"Bilingualism causes delays in language development" is probably the most common myth about bilingualism or multilingualism. As soon as you announce that you are going to teach your son or daughter a second language, or get caught "red-handed" doing so, the first and foremost concern, usually expressed in quite an aggressive manner, is that your child will suffer delays in language development. Sometimes you won't have any issues, so you'll just shrug it off and move on, not thinking about it a second time. But sometimes, your child will indeed have language development difficulties. Maybe your son or daughter is still not speaking at two or even three years old. Then you start wondering, "Maybe they were right. Maybe I shouldn't have packed so much into his language pool all at once." You start doubting yourself and decide to stop teaching your child a second language.

But let me assure you,
this myth couldn't be further from the truth.

While many may worry that raising a bilingual child will set them up for a delay in language development, studies have not found this to be the case. On the contrary, a large body of research indicates that bilingualism has numerous mental benefits in addition to the more obvious economic and practical ones. Bilingual children's language development, like their exposure to language, is split between their two languages. Learning a language as a monolingual or bilingual person has many similarities, but there are also big differences. Language development delays are not related to how many languages you speak. They have more physiological and psychological roots. So, if you insist on blaming the language development delays on bilingualism, then you are actually doing more harm than good because you are in denial and avoiding the actual root cause of the problem.

Inadequate Proficiency in Either Language

"Teaching your child multiple languages will result in failure in mastering any of them." - Similar to the previous myth, many people who don't know much about languages think that being bilingual or multilingual will slow down a child's overall language development and that your child won't be able to learn any of the languages well. They seem to think that children learn languages the same way adults do, but children's brains are still developing, and adults' brains are already fully formed. So how can this be similar? It is generally believed that children who learn two languages simultaneously during infancy go through a stage in which they are unable to distinguish between the two languages.

Evidence from all around the world has shown that this is not the case. In 1989, Cambridge University looked closely at the evidence for these claims [10]. It is said that bilingual children develop different language systems from birth, which lets them know when a *language switch* is happening very early on, and that they can use their developing languages in different ways depending on the situation. Do not worry that your child may get confused by learning two or more languages. Keep in mind that their brains are flexible, and the value of the skills they pick up in addition to learning a new language is priceless.

Children who are bilingual have an appreciation for the universality of objects despite their seemingly disparate names in each language they speak (object permanence). A "fish" represents a small animal that swims in water in both English and French, whether it is spelled "*fish*" or "*poisson*". When children are raised bilingual from early on, they will have an automatic perception of the meaning of the words they hear, without the need for mental translation from their mother tongue to a foreign language (this is how most children, who begin learning a foreign language after the golden period, tend to think).

Learning a new language has also been shown to improve analytical thinking, creativity, and cognitive flexibility. When children are exposed to multiple languages early and often, they grow up to be able to speak both or more languages at the same level of mastery and fluency. What's important is to keep all the languages active throughout the child's life. We must have faith in the magic of how children's brains develop, but this faith is strongly supported by evidence and science. It has the capacity to absorb, to remember, and to learn all that and more.

> *The brain is like a muscle –*
> *if you don't "exercise" it, it will "shrink".*

If we limit our child's development by underestimating his or her brain power, the brain will eventually stop stretching and settle for less, which will make learning harder in the future. You, as their parent, will need to invest considerable time in helping them do their homework. So, give your child what's best, take care of it properly, and you will see that your efforts do yield fruitful results.

Mixing Languages Is Bad

Bilingual people are characterized by their tendency

to blend languages when speaking. Unlike common beliefs, language mixing is a complex, rule-governed phenomenon, as stated by researchers Roberto Ramrez Heredia from Texas A&M International University and Jeanette Altarriba from State University of New York [11, 12]. The word-internal level is a common place where speakers of different languages blend their languages together, revealing how well the two grammars work together in the mind of the speaker. I have come into contact with a fair number of parents, or rather moms, who decided to stop teaching their children a second language as soon as they noticed the child was mixing languages. For example, when the mom asked a question in language A, the child answered in language B or mainly in language A with a few words from language B, it worried the mom that the child was not able to distinguish between the two languages, so she decided to stop bilingualism altogether. What a shame!

Mixing languages (also referred to as *code mixing*) is not bad at all; it is a natural phase for any child on their journey to bilingualism and multilingualism. That is how they learn! If being bilingual does affect the parts of the brain that are involved in cognitive control, task switching is then one of the human functions that is most affected. *Task switching* means switching from one set of rules to another quickly in response to changes in the environment. This is because bilingual people often switch tasks naturally, just like when they switch languages. Bilingual kids learn two sets of vocabulary; they have twice the number of words and twice the number of language rule sets to learn compared to their monolingual peers. When children try to express themselves, they usually use the vocabulary that they are familiar with. As a result, if they forget or don't know a word in one language, they will substitute it with the other language.

The important thing
is that they keep communicating.

Today, your child might mix up two languages by answering you in the "wrong" language because they don't yet know how to say it in the other language, but they are still expressing to you what they want to say. This is a good thing because communication is not broken. What you should then do is repeat what they said in the "right" language, slowly and clearly but casually, so they can learn how to say it in both languages without making a big deal out of "the mistake". For example, your child says "Mummy, I want uống nước". When that happens (which tends to be quite often with multilinguals), refrain at all costs from criticizing your child for mixing languages. Simply smile and repeat their sentence "correctly": "Oh you want to drink some water?" or "Con muốn uống nước hả?". Thanks to this way of reacting on a regular basis, your child will enjoy the benefits of a natural self-correcting process without feeling intimidated for saying the "wrong" thing.

What should you do if they mix up the languages again, even though you have already shown them how to say it in both languages? If you think about it, they might know how to say something in both languages, and they choose to do so in both, as a way of practice. There is another good thing that might be happening right there, and that is your child learning to indirectly *translate*. The ability to translate is non-arguably a vital skill for bilinguals and multilinguals as they will be put in the position of *implicit translator* sooner or later. Many adults (and children) who are bilingual frequently code switch while speaking, as is discussed later in this book. Numerous studies have shown that bilinguals' early exposure to alternating between their languages leads to the activation of brain areas involved in language control even when the individual is engaged in a non-linguistic cognitive task.

Boredom At School

"Learning a foreign language will make your child bored at school" - does it sound wrong just to me or to you too? You instill something interesting in your child from early on and you expect him or her to be bored at learning even more new and interesting things at school using the medium they are already familiar with? I know a lot of Vietnamese parents who claim that if the child masters English too early, then they will be bored during English classes when they start school. This is like saying "don't show them the meeting agenda beforehand or they will be bored during the actual meeting". Isn't it more appropriate and common practice to send the agenda of a meeting to all the attendees way before the scheduled meeting so they are more prepared and the meeting ends up more productive and effective?

I have a nephew who is six and a half who is Vietnamese with Vietnamese parents, living in Vietnam. Before staring the first grade, he had learned a decent amount of English from teachers, flashcards, TV shows, and books. At the age of six, he could already read both Vietnamese and English. Do you think that reading is the only thing that he would learn in the first grade? On the contrary, he would be excited to show off what he already knew and eager to learn more interesting new things.

Learning another language early on will boost your child's brain development and a whole lot of other skills like concentration, social skills, interest in reading, communication skills, and all that will help them perform better at school, not worse. Studies have shown that learning a foreign language early in life makes you smarter and helps you do better in other subjects, which means your child will also do better on reading and math tests.

Studies have shown that students who speak more than one language do better on standard tests for getting into college than monolingual students. US college entrance examination board back in 1998 already found that students who had studied a foreign language for four or more years on average did better on the verbal section of the SAT than those who had studied four or more years in any other subject. So don't worry, your academically brilliant and bilingual child will not be bored. If he is, then think about moving him to a better school, not cutting down on his early education.

Parents' Language Skills

"You can't teach your child a foreign language if you're not a native speaker" - many might loudly say, including yourself - the one reading this book right now. One of the common remarks I receive is that because my English is close to native, both in fluency and pronunciation, it is natural that my son will learn English well from an early age. This is not wrong because my linguistic privilege allows me to teach my son multiple languages better than an average Vietnamese person. Having said that, you can absolutely teach your child a second language even if you are not a native speaker. Even if you make mistakes in speaking English as a second language, it's still okay. Your child's magical brain powers allow him to modify and self-correct any mistakes that he would pick up from you or any other person through a wide range of exposure to different sources of the same language. You might think, "What if they think that my way is right and the right way is wrong?". Well, I don't have a ready answer to that because it doesn't happen. What you need to do is create the right support system, or the right linguistic environment, and your child will pick these things up naturally. When children are exposed to a foreign or second language at a young age, it helps them develop an "ear" for the language, which helps them speak and write it better as adults.

When children learn a foreign language, they have to figure out what words mean based on very different sounds. Some studies show that children who learn a second language before they turn thirteen are more likely to achieve native-like pronunciation. Remember how I mentioned earlier about the little element of faith that we ought to put in the process of acquiring bilingualism? How children learn a new language in the first six years of their lives is truly magical. It is not like you and I going to a language center, having paid heaps of money, and having class after class practicing grammar, reading, speaking, and writing. Children learn these things subconsciously in a natural environment, and it's amazingly effective.

What I'm trying to say is that if you understand a second language and you can speak full sentences in that language, then please do speak that language to your child under whatever strategy or principle you choose (I will introduce these principles later in this book). Expose your child to that language as early as possible to allow him to know at least as much as you know of that language. Then, be mindful about surrounding him with an appropriate linguistic environment and rest assured that he will pick up from there; he will self-correct, and his second language will keep developing until he achieves a desired level of fluency.

Passive Language Learning

Can you become bilingual simply by watching TV in multiple languages? Sure, you can learn to understand a second language from watching TV, reading books, listening to the radio or podcasts, listening to songs in multiple languages; but to be able to communicate in that language, hence being bilingual in its truest sense, *human interaction* is needed. A major reason for this is that, through active communication in different languages, your child develops a sense of empathy and emotional connection with these languages. A study in Psychology and Behavioral Sciences found in 2016 that children who speak more than one language are better at "putting themselves in other people's shoes" and understanding different points of view [13]. Bilingualism requires not only language skills but also the ability to understand the other speaker's perspective. Passive language learning is very different from bilingualism.

To achieve the level of proficiency bilinguals, the process of learning involves trial and error, making mistakes, mixing languages, and getting frustrated over not knowing how to express your thoughts or emotions in different languages.

We can see that all of these are very *active* ways of communicating, while watching TV or any other form of passive language absorption is, by nature, *passive*. With passive learning, you can learn to understand the words when you hear them, but as soon as you are required to verbally communicate with another person or group of people in that language, you stumble. It is because you are used to hearing, seeing, and receiving the phrases and sentences *passively* without having to form them in your head or pronounce them out loud.

> *I can be quite sure that if you (the one reading this book right now) are Vietnamese, you will have met a student who has studied English for many years, achieved exemplary grades in the subject, with perfect knowledge of grammar and vocabulary, but is unable to converse in English for more than five minutes without stumbling or turning red like a beetroot.*

All they do in those English classes is go through

chapters in their grammar books, filling in the blanks and writing the correct forms of verbs and tenses, without many chances to practice their perfect grammar in a long-form conversation. Even when it comes to reading books, no reading app can beat mom's lap and voice. So, while there are many good quality TV programs for very young children to learn different languages nowadays, it is inevitable to include *human interaction* as the major component of the learning process.

INTERESTING FACTS
ABOUT MULTILINGUALISM

Strategic Language Mixing

Multilinguals mix languages strategically; it is not random. I grew up in a multilingual environment, so most of my childhood friends were also multilingual. I didn't realize it at the time, but we always mixed languages when we talked to each other. Most of my friends in Poland were of Vietnamese descent, so they spoke Vietnamese to varying degrees, depending on the level of exposure to the minority language they had at home. They also went to Polish schools where general subjects were taught in Polish, but students also learned one or two foreign languages, being English and/or German. With time, we grew up to be able to command all the languages that we acquired simultaneously. When we talked to each other, we usually mixed different words from different languages here and there, and even though it felt random at the time, as I learned later, it really wasn't. We were absolutely able to converse entirely in one language, but we still chose to do it in multiple languages, whichever one felt the most comfortable and most natural in different parts of a conversation. When we talked to a monolingual, we usually had no problem expressing what we meant in a single language. To me, mixing languages was (and still is) like having a secret code for talking with my multilingual friends. *I feel free.* I feel as though I can express all my thoughts and feelings not only verbally but also emotionally. The level of emotion and connection that I form with the conversation and the people is maximized by mixing languages with those who understand those same languages.

Moreover, each language on this planet is characterized by different nuances. What you say in Spanish to express how you feel about a situation, when translated to English, often loses its true and full meaning. An example close to my heart would be the novel "A Hundred Years of Solitude" by Gabriel García Marquez, which was originally written in Spanish and regarded as one of the best novels of all time. Despite having studied Spanish, my Spanish proficiency is insufficient to read this novel in its original form (Spanish), so I had to read the English translation. But when translated into English, the novel somehow loses touch with the original regardless of how capable the translator is. This has been the shared opinion among many readers, especially the ones that are lucky enough to be able to read the novel in both Spanish and English.

So, to those who think that mixing languages is just a lazy or confused way of communicating: *well, it is quite the opposite*. Multilingual people are more than capable of conducting the same conversation in three or even more languages at an equal level of fluency; they just choose to add more color, depth, and meaning to their conversation by expressing each part of the conversation in the language that does it best. Mixing languages, which is also called "code mixing", is not a bad thing at all. In fact, it is normal for anyone on their way to becoming bilingual or multilingual.

Thinking in Different Languages

Multilinguals can think in different languages without translating their thoughts. If I got a dollar for every time someone asked me what language I think in or whether I translate from one language to another when I think about something, I would probably be very rich right now. And the answer to the latter is "*No, I don't.*" When I think in Vietnamese, I think in Vietnamese. When I think in English, I think in English. And when I think in Polish, I think in Polish. I don't translate between languages in my head. This is quite similar to the mixing of the languages that I discussed in the previous section. Just like mixing languages in a verbal conversation with another multilingual, the thoughts inside my head are like the conversation I have with myself. So, whichever language I feel most comfortable expressing my thoughts in my head, that's the language that I will think in.

This is a skill that most bilingual and multilingual people have - especially those that acquired multiple languages as very young children, this incredible skill becomes effortless. Many multilinguals have a preference for one language over the others (perhaps due to its frequent use or highest emotional connection), but they are still able to think in each of the languages separately. A person who learns a second language through passive language learning or inadequate/infrequent exposure usually thinks in their mother tongue and then translates that thought into whatever language they are having a conversation in. This disrupts the flow and quality of communication because it takes time and energy to translate, regardless of whether it is translating your own thoughts in your head or translating what the other person said.

If you think about it, this is quite magical. Becoming multilingual does not only give you the ability to speak and communicate in different languages, but it also changes something in your brain that allows you to formulate thoughts and ideas in different languages. *That something* is commonly referred to as "cognitive muscle". It is responsible for focus and decision making. By learning multiple languages simultaneously, young children develop their own cognitive flexibility. Researchers have found that the brains of bilingual and multilingual children develop more densely. This may be one reason why learning a second language is good for your brain. Wellcome Centre for Human Neuroimaging in London with experts from the Fondazione Santa Lucia in Rome [14], used brain imaging to find that bilingual speakers had denser grey matter than monolingual study participants. Brains are like muscles. Children's brains develop at a rapid pace in their early years. During the first six years, ninety percent of their brains are formed. Bilingual children, who receive language exposure from day one, are able to detect *language switch* as early as six months old (which means they know when mom is speaking Vietnamese and when she's speaking English). This is when they form and continue to build their respective language rulesets. Most babies aren't yet talking at six months old, but they sure understand the idea of different languages [15]. How amazing is that?

Academic Performance at School

Bilingual children acquire two phonological systems

and thus receive additional "practice" in the sounds of different languages. Importantly, studies show that phonological awareness skills (which is being aware of and able to work with the sounds in spoken language - the foundation for decoding, blending, and, eventually, reading words) are easily transferred from one language to another in bilingual children. Researchers at American University led by Dr Jennifer Steele [16] found that at the end of secondary school, students who were exposed to two languages at home had gained an academic year's worth of knowledge in English reading compared to their monolingual peers. Given adequate exposure to both languages in the early years, bilingual children are able to master them and perform well on quantitative tests in both languages, at least as well as monolingual children. By the time your child is six years old, he or she only needs approximately a third of overall exposure to each language over time compared to a monolingual peer to score the same on standard tests in each of the two languages.

The benefits of bilingual education have been studied for thirty years by George Mason University professors Wayne Thomas and Virginia Collier [17]. Somewhat better test scores and a general sense of school satisfaction have been seen among bilingual students compared to their English-only and one-way immersion peers in studies spanning six US states and thirty seven districts. Parents are more involved, students are more regular in showing up to class, and behavioral issues are less frequent. It was also found that bilingual children are more successful at and enjoy solving mental puzzles compared to their monolingual friends. Research conducted in 2008 by psychologists Ellen Bialystok and Michelle Martin-Rhee discovered that when comparing monolingual and bilingual children, the bilinguals were better able to sort objects based on shape and color [18]. This indicates that being bilingual enhances the ability to follow instructions and carry out activities such as planning and problem solving. As Gigi Luk, a Harvard professor, said: "Bilingualism is an experience that shapes our brains for a lifetime."

Bilingualism Is A Shortcut To Biculturalism

Despite their frequent co-occurrence, "bicultural" and "bilingual" do not refer to the same thing. There is a clear divide between fluency (cultural competence or knowledge) and use (interacting in two or more cultures) when defining a "bicultural" individual, even among the limited number of classifications that do exist. In 2008, when writing that bilinguals "have two different and full sets" of knowledge structures, one for each culture, David Luna from the University of Central Florida, Torsten Ringberg from Copenhagen Business School, and Laura Peracchio from the University of Wisconsin Milwaukee appeared to place the focus on the *equivalency of fluency* [19]. Bilingualism does not equate to biculturalism, but with a background in the language of another culture, you'll have easier access to communities all over the world. Learning a second language lets you talk to people from other cultures and gives you access to a whole network of people you might not have met before. It's important nowadays to have cosmopolitan people in "a melting pot society", especially in light of ever-increasing global integration and digitization of economies.

In today's globalized world, being able to speak more than one language is becoming more and more important. When applying for a job, bilingual candidates can differentiate themselves from other candidates by showcasing their invaluable language, communication, and cognitive skills. Knowing a foreign language can be the unique talent that gets you that first or final interview, says James Doherty of Winter Wyman Contract Staffing. People from different countries and cultures must find ways to communicate with each other in a society that is becoming more and more diverse. As Kathleen Marcos said, "Society as a whole also benefits economically, politically, and socially when its people can communicate with and appreciate people from other countries and cultures." Our children will live in a better world if people are open, aware, empathetic, and appreciate the value of different cultures and languages. So, even though bilingualism does not equate to biculturalism, it is definitely a fast lane to it.

Simultaneous Language Acquisition

The key is in your approach and execution. Children can absolutely learn two or more languages simultaneously, even when taught exclusively by one parent (you). The first critical factor is that *you complete a full sentence in each of the languages*. Never combine multiple languages in one sentence - this is what increases the amount and severity of language confusion, which will take your child longer to self-correct. The second critical factor is that *you use two or more languages simultaneously*. What I mean is that you should say everyday sentences like "Would you like a glass of water?" in English, then "Con có muốn uống nước không?" in Vietnamese (or any other language that you are teaching them) one after the other. Never say "Con có muốn water không?" which has the same meaning, but you used two different languages in the same sentence. Or, instead of saying "Đây là cái bus", say "This is a bus" or "Đây là xe buýt". I have heard so many parents say this exact sentence to their children in Vietnam (i.e. "Đây là cái bus", "Đây là màu blue"). While your child will eventually learn the difference between the two languages, it will take them much longer if their bilingual exposure is a constant blend of "potpourri".

Research shows that bilingual children learn the

structures of each of their languages in a way that is similar to how a single language is learned, as suggested by Elin Thordardottir, a professor at McGill University in Canada. However, there are also structures that are unique to bilingualism, which suggests that the languages are learned independently most of the time, but not always. With both sets of vocabulary taken into account, there is a general consensus among researchers that when it comes to early vocabulary, *simultaneously bilingual* children develop in a way that is similar to that of monolingual children [20, 21]. This suggests that children are capable of absorbing multiple languages at the same time with equally successful outcomes (i.e., being multilingual). In other words, learning more than one language will not negatively affect your child's overall language learning. Occasional confusion and language mixing are all part of a very normal process of becoming multilingual. Parents should embrace these hurdles as part of a wonderful journey towards multilingualism and an unlimited world of opportunities for their children.

FOUNDATIONS FOR MULTILINGUALISM
IN A MONOLINGUAL ENVIRONMENT

We have now discussed the science behind multilingualism, common strategies, myths, and facts about multilingualism. According to a widely shared opinion, the "time and place" strategy is the most difficult one to implement, but also the one holding the most power for natural bilingualism. The other two strategies - "one person, one language" and "minority language at home" - are quite widely implemented and quite successfully too. But what about raising a multilingual child in a monolingual environment? It is not applicable to any of the above strategies, and it is what most of us parents living in our home countries desire while striving to help our children speak English fluently and correctly from an early age.

My personal situation is a perfect example of this. I used to live in several different countries, but now I live in Vietnam. My son was born in Vietnam and will most likely stay in Vietnam at least until university. Everybody around us is Vietnamese. The entire immediate and extended family speaks Vietnamese only. Nobody other than me (the mother) and my brother (the uncle) are fluent in English. And since my brother lives abroad, that leaves only me as a source of proper English language instruction for my son. So, what strategy should I adopt? How to best give my son the gift of multilingualism?

I mentioned earlier that I would tell you why the commonly known strategies for raising bilingual children would not work for us. Here is why. The "one parent, one language" strategy would not work because if I spoke only English at home, my husband would not understand it. I also want my child to know that I can speak Vietnamese and that he can speak Vietnamese to me because we are, in fact, Vietnamese nationals. I wouldn't want to teach him English at the price of losing our cultural heritage.

But I also want my son to be able to communicate in English freely, effortlessly, and natively. My husband doesn't speak English, so he is only able to communicate with my son in Vietnamese, and that's precisely what I ask of my husband: speak proper Vietnamese to our son – always. My husband learns new English words here and there, and he tries to say them to my son, but understandably the pronunciation is not perfect, as he is essentially a novice learner. I politely asked him to speak to our son only in Vietnamese so as not to teach him the wrong way to pronounce English. The "minority language at home" strategy would not work either, because outside of our home, people use Vietnamese all around us, while at home, at least his father always uses Vietnamese. I also use Vietnamese when speaking to my husband and half the time when speaking to my son, so it's not possible for us to use English at home and Vietnamese outside of the home. The "time and place" strategy is out the window for us as well, for practicality reasons.

So, how should I do it? *Of course, I invented my own method.* Rather than being strictly rule-based, this method is more of a *flexible, adaptive, self-evolving* process. The following three foundations firmly underlie my three golden principles (discussed in the next chapter) that constitute my very own strategy for raising bilingual children in non-bilingual environments. You are welcome to read it, absorb it, dissect it, modify it, and apply your own version of it to your family.

Our (yours and mine) goal is one and the same:
to give our precious children
the invaluable gift of multilingualism for life.

Foundation One:
Use Languages Simultaneously

The two languages that you're trying to instill should be spoken to your child in a natural manner, such as during daily activities, during trips to the zoo, trips to the supermarket, and casual questions during the day, such as "what colour is this?", "what shape is that?", "what animal is it?", "what should you do when it rains?", "what do we have to put on our heads when we ride a bike?", among many other daily questions. Little things like that should be conducted as much as possible in both languages simultaneously. You would say something in Vietnamese first or English first and then immediately repeat it in the other language. This is not in accordance with either of the commonly known strategies for raising bilingual kids; it is rather a mixture of all the strategies combined with a pinch of common sense. It is what has essentially evolved from the way I've been raising my son, who is already quite confidently bilingual at age three.

Use both languages simultaneously, but only when it makes sense, which should be majority of the time, except sometimes your child's mood can be quite cranky or sensitive and it just doesn't make sense to be too stringent about bilingualism in those moments. But the more important thing is to maintain your child's *interest* in using the language, so ideally, I would suggest using both languages simultaneously during exciting activities such as going to the museum, colouring with mom at home, or other things that spark excitement, because that is when their brains are the most receptive.

Children who are simultaneously bilingual are exposed to both languages when they are babies and young children. Since these children are exposed to more than one language, they get less total exposure to each language compared to monolinguals. Because of this difference in exposure, a bilingual child's knowledge of each language is not the same. Also, bilingual children are exposed to a wider range of language structures than monolinguals. Even though they hear each language less, research has shown that many bilingual children are able to overcome this problem and develop language systems that are similar to those of their monolingual peers, at least in one language or in both.

A lot of people feel like the early years are just for eating, sleeping, and playing. This is not wrong because they are going through incredible amounts of physical growth. And while most children are not yet capable of working on a big scientific project by NASA at the age of four, they are able to get involved in "play", which is essentially the work of a child according to Maria Montessori. As parents, our role is to facilitate the kinds of activities and XXXinteractions that will enhance brain development in the early years of our children's lives. Instead of sitting your child in front of a TV or sending him off to a playground, day after day, try out some ideas and get involved in your child's play. Design some sensory activities to boost their creativity and spark their joy, excitement, and interest. *Be involved.*

Never underestimate the power of
simply being present.

Choose to include multiple languages in some of the activities. While I understand that parents need rest, you shouldn't always treat your child's playtime as your "downtime". You can have fun playing with your children too. Calm your mind, set your to-do list aside, focus on the present. Something that children can teach us is *to live in the moment, be present,* and *notice the little things.* Mould some play dough together, watch clouds in the sky, make paper planes, paint some masks, build a sandcastle, draw an abstract painting, and include multiple languages as you do these. But make sure you use each language on its own in a *full sentence*. If this is too demanding for you linguistically, just name things in different languages without forming full sentences. This will work too, but you will soon notice your child's inquiries about how to use those words in full sentences when they try to express themselves.

Foundation Two:
Follow Your Child's Lead

Even though I do emphasize the importance of interest right in this chapter, I urge you to follow your child's *lead* instead of your child's *interest*. How are they different? – you might ask. Most of the time, these two will overlap. However, sometimes curiosity prevails and what usually interests your child would not be their choice in a particular moment. Whichever language I choose to teach my son in, I make sure that it stems from my son's lead rather than from a "curriculum". I firmly believe that only when he is interested in something will he effectively and fully absorb anything new that is taught to him in relation to that topic. Sometimes, this means that even when I am asking him about the colour of a tomato, and he suddenly seems as if he did not hear me and he wants to act like a wolf, my best course of action in this moment will be to play along and talk about the wolf in both languages – maybe the colour, the size, or the sound of the wolf – so that his mind absorbs this new information, because if I stay fixated on the tomato, I will lose the opportunity to talk with him about the wolf, as well as colours, shapes, and sounds. This applies to learning anything but is particularly applicable to learning languages because *immediate interest*, hence *lead*, is the most important factor in how effective language learning is going to be. If you think a movie is boring but you keep watching it until the end, you will still roughly know the story line. But if a language is boring you and you still must learn it forcefully, your brain will essentially ignore it.

Children could be interested in anything, in theory.

Studies have been done on boys' and girls' interests since the early 1900s. This information was used to figure out what books or activities teachers might want to assign to their students. More recent studies of interest content have focused on the types of interests, where they come from, how much they are related to school, and the range and intensity of interests. Findings show that interests can be described in terms of leisure, school, and work; students' interests usually start at home; and interests are often not related to school. Also, different children are interested in different things, so one child's interest is not likely to be the same as another's. Children and students in elementary school are influenced by the other kids and students around them. Teachers, parents, and other kids all have direct and indirect effects on what classes to take and what toys to play with, as well as what classes and toys are available. In fact, differences in interests based on gender start to show up around age three, and from then on, children decide for themselves which interests are "appropriate" and which are not. Even though people tend to stay interested in the same things for a long time, kids are always finding new things to like, and the things they already like are always being combined or merged into new things.

Children's interest development has been linked to the questions and challenges of play, the influence of others, and figuring out what gender they are. Young children's changing understandings and what could be called "reciprocal self-knowledge" seem to be an important part of how their interests grow. The study of young children's free play, for example, shows that both girls and boys will try out things like balancing and sequencing. They will also use more strategies and more patterns of activity when playing and working with things they are interested in than with things they are not. In fact, researchers have said that children at this age develop based on what interests them. This is why I want to reiterate that parents should follow their child's lead instead of (presumed) interest. Interest is extremely important, but it is not constant, especially as children grow. So instead of assuming what your child will like, choose to be more observant and mindful about what interests your child in a given moment.

Foundation Three:
Show Positive Associations

In my case, my son will be natively fluent in Vietnamese no matter what. Everybody around him speaks Vietnamese, he will go to school with Vietnamese children, he will encounter Vietnamese at restaurants, supermarkets, or playgrounds. English, on the other hand, is the secondary language that I strive to pass on to him alongside Vietnamese. Without making too big of a deal about speaking English in his eyes, I try to give him positive associations with English so that he enjoys learning it, hearing it, and speaking it. Only through practice will he be able to actually use the language.

So, if we make learning English a chore, something forced, something that a child feels like they are doing just to please mom, then we have defeated the purpose. Almost all the fun activities, like dancing, singing, reciting poems, doing puzzles, learning about animals, and playing games, can easily be done in English. In the midst of all the fun, we shouldn't forget to say things in Vietnamese as well. But if most of the fun is in English, then the child will associate English with fun, and thus will enjoy learning it.

At three years and four months of age, my son loves to play make-believe and role-play where all his made-up conversations and monologues are in English. He then tells him dad what happens in his made-up story in Vietnamese. When he stumbles, he often looks to me for assistance with vocabulary – and I help him so he can tell his dad all about his play. This dynamic always seems to make him very happy and proud of himself. He then goes off to play and imagine some more, be it in English or Vietnamese. It also makes my heart very full because I can see that my efforts do pay off.

GOLDEN PRINCIPLES FOR
MULTILINGUAL PARENTING

With the above-described foundations in mind, I have developed my own strategy for raising my child as bilingual in a non-bilingual environment: my Golden Principles for Multilingual Parenting. Feel free to take what you need from them and use the rest to shape your own approach to parenting. You and I both just want to provide our children with the lifelong gift of multilingualism. This chapter is perhaps the jist of this book, a devotion from my heart and soul. With the goal being that my child grows effortlessly bilingual and develops the ability to communicate natively and fluently in both languages, whichever ones you choose, the following three principles are what I live by when raising my son. I call these: My Golden Principles for Multilingual Parenting.

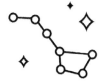

Principle One:
Language Exposure

Repetitive, frequent, and constant language exposure. The biggest obstacle that parents (who know English) need to overcome to teach their children another language is the feeling of shyness when speaking a non-native language with them. When your child is still a newborn, spend a couple of months talking to them every day, just one or two sentences in English (the second language that you are trying to teach them), while the rest of the interaction can still be in your native language, to gradually reduce your own shyness. The earlier you start, the better. Note that in the first few months of your child's life, their linguistic comprehension is limited, so this is your chance to "practice" speaking two languages to your child without any real consequences. When your child becomes a toddler and starts to imitate your words, then it becomes a little harder to "practice".

I remember, as fluent as I am in English, I still found it awkward to speak in English to my newborn, especially being a first-time mom. So I started with a simple "good morning, sunshine" every single morning, and "time to take a bath, splash splash" every single afternoon before his bath. Each day, I would consciously say more and more phrases in English. By the time my son was 6 months old, I felt no shyness whatsoever about speaking in English to him at home or in public (note that at 6 months old, kids are not talking yet, so it was just me talking monologue to my baby in both Vietnamese and English). As they grow older and you speak more and more to them, try to increase the amount of English to at least a third of your wake-time interaction with your child. This is all to give your child an invaluable gift: the ability to be multilingual. The benefits of multilingualism have been detailed earlier in this book to quite a great extent.

Language exposure, which is repetitive, frequent, and constant, means that you are not just teaching your child what an apple is called in English, or Spanish, or whichever language. Your focus should not be on the memorization of words but rather on exposing your child to both languages in a natural environment. For example, daily activities, playtime, bathtime, mealtime, outings. The key is "language exposure," but it must be repetitive, frequent, and constant. Furthermore, the exposure must be in both desired languages without diluting them. Say things like the following, but in both (or more) languages to your child on a daily basis, whenever appropriate:

"Hold on a second"

"Would you like this one or that one?"

"Again? One more time?"

"Do you want to go over there?"

"Here you are, say please/thank you."

For the most part, anything I say to my son in Vietnamese, I will also repeat in English. I am the type of mom who sees immense educational value in certain Youtube shows such as Super Simple Songs, Little Baby Bum, Blippi, or Peppa Pig, Paw Patrol,

Bluey, Teletubbies, and many others. All the shows and channels that I put on for my son in the early years are strictly in proper English and carefully selected in terms of content. During screen time, he either watches something that he has already watched before (which I had approved of) or if he wants to watch something new, I will sit with him and watch the entire thing with him to make sure there is adequate educational value in it. The last thing I would want is to waste screen time on nonsensical content.

I was asked more than once about my son's screen time and how much of it he gets each day. My answer has always been, "We don't have a screen time rule at home. He can watch his shows when he wants, just like he can go play with his Lego when he wants." I could see a surprised expression on all their faces, and I could also feel a sense of judgement towards me. Unlimited screen time? That's just permissive parenting. Nope, I do that very consciously. I don't make a big deal out of "watching TV" because I don't want it to be seen as a "reward" by my son. The more you forbid or restrict access to something, the more desirable it becomes. What I do instead is watch it with him, or at least interact every now and then in relation to something from the show he's watching, like "That is one funny elephant, huh?". The key to avoiding TV addiction is not letting your child lose himself in the aimless passiveness of the activity. Instead, your child should feel excited because he is learning something interesting, like a new song, the alphabet, or animal sounds. One way to achieve that is to include what he watches on TV in your daily life. Align the TV shows that you allow him to watch with his current interests. In other words, use TV as an educational tool in parenting rather than a mindless bribe (reward) or your own downtime.

The biggest obstacle for parents like me, who can speak multiple languages but are not part of a multicultural family and wish to pass the multiple languages on to their children, is the feeling of shyness when speaking a non-native language with their child, as mentioned earlier. Your role is critical, and you must first overcome this feeling. You must feel comfortable speaking another language to your child. It is the only way that you will persist through the tough times and commit to multilingual parenting for the long haul. Take one or two months, during which you commit to saying one or two simple sentences a day to your child. This gradual transition should make it easier for you to increase the amount of language exposure as your child grows older. If you can do that, you will be giving your child an invaluable gift for life: multilingualism.

This is most easily and effectively done in the first six years of your child's life, with the biggest portion of development happening in the first three years. We must remember that we are not attempting to convert our children to be American or British. We are attempting to equip our children with better "tools" for the future by teaching them to communicate in two or more languages. Although the first six years of life are critical for subconscious language development, it is important to remember that we do not have to teach our child everything there is to know about either of these languages in the first six years of life. No, we want to lay a solid foundation for them to build on as they grow older. At the same time, make certain that you do not teach them any of the languages incorrectly. Try not to overcomplicate it. Whatever you teach him, keep it simple at first, then elaborate as your child's abilities develop.

Repetition is key.

Let's look at an example. You take your child to the playground, and there are slides, swings, and seesaws. This setting presents an opportunity for you to practice using both languages with your child. Keep in mind that if you are significantly more fluent in Vietnamese while your English is elementary, don't think that you must forcefully use English the whole time you are at the playground. Every now and then, a couple of words is enough. For example, when your child slides down the slide and wants to go up and slide again, after verbalizing your child's desire in Vietnamese, you can reinforce it once again in English. No need for the whole sentence translation, just "slide again?" is enough. Very short phrases, very short words are sufficient yet so powerful, because that is when your child is listening with *full attention*. The activity of sliding down is kind of an accomplishment for your child, so they would usually be looking at you for a reaction or compliment as soon as they slide down - an applause, a smile, anything to let them know they are seen and valued. That is your window of opportunity for *highly sensitive language absorption.* You can use that window of focus to speak English. When they answer you, they might say "yes" in Vietnamese, which again you might want to reinforce in English - "yes". Never tell your child directly and right away that they are wrong, especially in such highly sensitive windows of focus. If you want your child to respond to you in English, you just need to repeat their Vietnamese statement of agreement in English - "yeah, let's slide again." And just like that, such short words, phrases, and sentences being repeated in both languages throughout the whole playground experience is enough to gradually build your child's English vocabulary and the way of using that vocabulary in a natural environment.

Another example is when you take a walk of fifteen minutes (or any amount of time) with your child, you have another opportunity to use both languages in a natural situation. Don't overthink it; just say very simple things like "This is a tree" in both languages while pointing at a tree. Encourage your toddler to point at a tree as well. You are likely to see more than one tree on your walk, so point it out in both languages any time you see it. "That's a car", "Oh look, a flower", or "The tree is so big, and the flower is so small". Relatively simple and practical, right? Without requiring extensive effort from the parent, these simple, short, and practical remarks have an enormous effect on the child's language development.

Despite being able to absorb new knowledge and languages like a sponge in their first six years of life, toddlers are still toddlers and are not yet able to handle complex, multi-layered language. Regardless of which language you are using with your child, primary or secondary, all the communication with them should be simple, to the point, without any need for logical elaboration. Learning languages is a subconscious (sometimes referred to as "unconscious" or "implicit") process for young children. The magic of unconscious language learning is truly miraculous, especially in young children. They can learn the complexities and irregularities of a foreign language without even realizing it.

Unconscious language learning doesn't mean that your child learns during sleep, but rather that your child just learns without realizing it. If you really think about it, this is perhaps one of the most interesting things that can happen to the mind: the ability to learn a language's complex and subtle patterns without even realizing it. In a child's first few years, this kind of "implicit" language learning seems to happen on its own. However, learning a second language as an adult is usually not easy and success rates vary.

Stephen Krashen, a linguist at the University of Southern California, found that there are two main ways to learn a language: through conscious "learning" and through subconscious "acquisition" [22]. Language learning usually involves following the rules of a new language. This is common in classrooms. Teachers teach students rules about grammar and how to say words, and then they show students how these rules work in real life. On the other hand, most people think of *immersive* language learning when they think of language acquisition. Imagine, for example, an immigrant child who spends hours each day with her peers and picks up (or "acquires") the new language. Krashen says that the best way to learn a language is to focus on learning the language rather than on grammar rules. When students are actively speaking and listening, they pay more attention to what is being said than to how it is being said. Students who are good at grammar know the rules, but they don't follow them when they speak. Instead, they have gotten a feel for the language, which helps them make sentences that flow better. Their knowledge of grammar is often used to make last-minute changes to what they say before they say it. People often refer to this part of the grammar as the "monitor" because it checks, reviews, and edits what the mind comes up with.

Language learning can occur through real time interactions with other people as well as subconscious listening during their quiet and independent playtime, like when they're playing with blocks or magnets, drawing, or colouring. It is a good idea to sometimes put on an audio file with an English story or recitation of English words or poems. This way, your child is focused on doing something with their hands and eyes, but their mind is secretly learning a foreign language. But this doesn't just apply to foreign languages. Subconscious listening can also be applied to the mother-tongue language. The most common way of using this method is through playing audio recordings of poems, short children's stories, and songs. It is important that these are audio files, not cartoons with visuals, because anything that is visual, colorful, and moving tends to attract the child's attention more than sounds. You certainly don't want their attention to be focused on the screen while your intentions are for language acquisition. Subconscious listening works as an implicit, indirect process while your child is calmly and peacefully focused on doing something else with their eyes and hands. Many adults prefer doing something with their hands that does not require thinking, like meditative coloring, running, or jogging, while listening to an audiobook or a podcast. We absorb the audio better when doing something with our hands. If our hands are idle (like when we're lying in bed at night), audiobooks (even the greatest classics) often work even better than lullabies in sending us right to sleep.

This is also why hiring an English language teacher, whether by inviting them to come to your house or by sending your child to a class, doesn't really work when your child is still very young, i.e., younger than six. The key at this stage is repetitive, frequent, and constant exposure to both languages, especially the secondary language. If you send your child to a class or invite a teacher to your home twice a week, three times a week, or even every day, that's just one to two hours each day at most. Not only is it insufficient because the remaining twenty-three hours are in a different language, it also brings unnecessary stress and pressure from forced learning. Your child is still forcefully learning the foreign language in a restricted window of time - this is very different from language acquisition in a natural environment. Their ability to master a second language will be significantly more restricted than their mother tongue. Of course, it's not a bad idea if you just want your child to have passive knowledge of the foreign language and then continue learning it in full swing once they start school. But in this book, I have poured my soul into something more intrinsic, more inherent, where you give your child the tools to navigate both languages equally with ease as they learn to speak. This is very different from adding a new language when one language is already formed. Through this book, I am determined to help you reduce the likelihood that your child will struggle to learn a second language at school.

Principle Two:
Books and Literature

Nurture the love for books and literature. No child is born with a dislike of reading. They learn it from adults who dislike reading. And there is no such thing as "dislike of reading" anyway. There is only you not having found a book that you like. Not all parenting books emphasize the importance of loving books. But in my eyes, books and literature are as important as parenting itself. Somewhere along life's hustles and bustles, many of us adults seem to let the inherent interest in books and storytelling slip away. Only in the most nostalgic moments do we ever revisit our childhood books and, thus, memories. Reading has become less of a priority as life takes over. Exploring our inner selves has become inferior to chasing materialistic goals. But books and reading are about much more than sheer pleasure. I see books as vitamins for the mind and soul. Idleness will result in staleness. As parents, the absence of our own reading will likely lead to minimal, if any, reading by our children.

Children do as you do, not as you say.

Experiments have shown that when adults and kids read books together, the kids can learn new words. Sénéchal and Cornell of the International Literacy Association found in 1993 that even a single reading of a book helps young children learn new words [23]. In the same way, according to the Journal of Educational Psychology, Robbins and Ehri found in 1994 that children could learn new words by listening to stories read twice without being told what the words meant [24]. Your child's request to read a single book over and over again actually has paramount benefits for their vocabulary development. I think I must have read "The Very Hungry Caterpillar" by Eric Carle out loud at least five hundred times (I'm not joking). Lacking a reading role model is a lack of communicating with your child that reading is fun. We, as adults, must consciously and purposely put in an effort to help our children love reading, enjoy choosing books to read, and associate reading with something positive and pleasant. There are ways to achieve that, even if you are not a bookworm. You can still create a habit and interest in reading for your child.

Something that has survived through time and turbulence of human evolution is literature.

When it comes to raising bilingual children in a non-bilingual environment, I cannot emphasize enough the importance of cultivating a love for reading books in your child. There is a saying that "a child who reads will grow up to be an adult who thinks," which is both true and inspiring at the same time. Books are the gatekeepers of all valuable knowledge. Even with current technological advancement and the evolution of online resources, the value of books has never subsided. Through a variety of sensory cues, reading helps children build foundational reading contexts that encourage active exploration and learning. Picture books in various interactive forms are by far the best way to teach kids to read. This is because they are made to engage children's senses, so they usually have different layouts and textures. As your child gets older, they can start to enjoy chapter books, which have more words and fewer pictures.

When you realize the importance of books and what you can learn through reading, then the sky is your limit. And yet, many of us choose to go the quicker and easier route to acquire knowledge, like watching a five-minute video online, reading a blog post, or talking to someone who might know something that we need. While all these methods are perfectly valid and effective ways to gain new knowledge, they lack profundity. We always seem to admire it when we see a child who holds a book and actually enjoys reading. These children seem to have a more curious mind than their average peers. We've got to realize that it doesn't just happen like that. Yes, some kids have that inner desire to read, but in one way or another, it was initiated by their parents or guardians. An exceptional example would be that of

Matilda by Roald Dahl. Her parents were negligent, and so was her headmaster, but she had one teacher who valued her uniqueness and nurtured her mind and abilities. Despite lacking family encouragement, she was driven to learn and was helped along the way by a single inspiring teacher. It is important to recognize, however, that Matilda is not the most commonly observed norm.

The way that kids behave generally stems from the way that their parents behave. So, whatever we want our children to do or whatever we want our children to be, we've got to lead by example. We want to see a child who reads, right? Then we've got to put the phone down and actually read something paper-based. You might read a newspaper or a magazine, a cookbook or a novel, a self-help book, or a biography. You can choose to read whatever your heart desires, but you've got to make sure that you don't read from an electronic device and that your child can see you reading actual books. In our adult eyes, reading on a Kindle or an app on your phone is the same as reading a physical book, which is a discussion for another time. In your child's eyes, there is a difference between holding a book and holding a phone, even if it's reading an ebook on your phone. We've got to be mindful and conscious about setting an example for our children.

When selecting books to read for your child, make sure that you get the fun books. They should be age-appropriate as well as aligned with your child's current interest/s (i.e., follow your child's lead). We have discussed "following your child's lead" quite extensively in the previous part of this book, and I would like to reiterate that because of its paramount importance. If you don't follow your child's lead, your good intentions might turn into forceful and close-minded parenting. Who's to say that your choice of books is better than the child-led choice anyway? It is important to create positive associations with reading for your child through story time. At the beginning, when the child is still small and doesn't really interact with you during story time, you can read any book to your child (like "The Harvard Business Review" or "War and Peace") and just prioritize instilling the action of holding a physical book next to your child and reading it out loud. You might choose to read something that is incomprehensible for your child, and that's okay because in the early months, the content doesn't really matter just yet. Some high-contrast board books that are black and white and designed for newborns might have a beneficial effect, but generally speaking, what is important is the consistency of reading a book with your child daily to create a habit and to show that reading is something normal and enjoyable. Whenever you hold a book and read it to your child, you should create a happy and positive atmosphere. Don't read a book when your child is crying, fussing, hungry, or needs a diaper change. Finish everything that needs to be finished first; address all of your child's physiological needs; make sure your child is comfortable and content; and then spend five to ten minutes each day just holding a book and reading it to your baby. After that, when the child is more communicative, interactive, able to touch and turn the pages, point at pictures, that's when you've got to be more selective and mindful with the books that you bring home for your child.

Usually, in the first two to three years of your child's life, the best choices are board books, which are not easily torn apart and allow your child to practice turning the thick cardboard pages as their fine motor skills are still developing. Otherwise, you might be spending a fortune repurchasing books because they get destroyed by your very active toddler. With consistency throughout the years, it is important to realise that it's okay to close and put away a book before finishing reading it; it's okay to turn the page before you've read all the lines; and it's okay to invent your own words instead of reading the book word for word. Books with vibrant colors are always a good choice. Pictures should not be too busy with details or too abstract, but rather simple and clearly relatable to real life are the most suitable, especially in the early years. It's very important that the parent understands that they don't have to finish reading a certain story to the child for the child to like reading books. Please take that pressure off yourself. Depending on the day, your child might not want to sit still and listen to a story for very long, or even not at all - it is okay. Maybe your child is not in the mood for reading or simply doesn't enjoy that particular story. Even the biggest bookworms are not always in the mood for reading. The key is to observe your child and adjust accordingly, following their lead and interests.

Your child will learn about the act of reading through observing how you hold a book, how you turn the pages, how you point at different pictures on the pages, and the expressions that you make with your voice and face. All of these will help the child associate reading books or story time with certain experiences. Pointing at different things on the pages is part of language development for your child, because through understanding the link between what you are showing with your finger, what you are saying out loud, and what you are expressing with your face as well as the tone of your voice, helps them understand the verbal part as well as the body language part of languages. Through reading books regularly, you are giving your child an invaluable opportunity to receive and enhance language development. In order to do this, you need to make sure that whichever language you are reading a book to your child in, you are pronouncing that language correctly. You don't want to set the wrong foundation for the secondary language, such as English. If you are not very confident in your own pronunciation, use the help of recorded audio by native speakers, which is usually available with your purchase of the physical books. But don't just turn on the audio and leave your child to it. Your presence and interaction become even more important when you are not reading the stories out loud yourself.

It is a good idea to change your facial expressions and the tone of your voice frequently as you read through the stories. You might want to do impressions of different characters in the stories, or when there are pictures of different animals in the book, you might want to stop and pretend that you are that animal and make the relevant animal sounds. This way, your child will be more interested in reading time because it's more fun. Try to avoid asking your child things that you know they don't know because this decreases their level of interest and confidence. Instead, encourage your child to repeat, say out loud, or point with their finger at things which you know for sure that they know and can pronounce. This works similarly to saying positive affirmations each morning before you start the day. When you can actually do something successfully or see that you are able to give correct answers, then deep inside yourself, you start believing that you are capable of a lot more. That is the level of self-confidence and optimism that you want to instill in your child.

The point is not to read all the words on the pages, but rather to help your child love the act of reading.

Instead of exhausting your child's interest in the story, try to stop story time before your child is bored. You can say, "That's all for today. We'll read more tomorrow, okay?" This helps your child associate reading time with a reward, something to look forward to; hence, they enjoy it more and more each time. At the age of two, I am proud to say, my son independently went to his bookshelf, chose a book he wanted to read, brought the book to me, and asked me to read it for him. When that book was finished, he took the book back to the bookshelf, chose another one, went to mommy and said, "mommy read book". At the age of three, he has a few favorite books which he keeps by our bedside, and he can "read" to me most lines in these books even though he can't actually read yet. My heart melts every single time. Not only because that is undeniably pure cuteness in itself, but also because I can see the result of my ongoing efforts so clearly right then and there. From a 5-month-old who did not give me much reaction or enthusiasm during story time to a now three-and-a-half-year-old who is so smart and enjoys reading books every single day.

What I'm trying to say is *be patient* - it doesn't happen instantly. For some kids, it does, but for most, it doesn't. I started reading to my baby when he was still in the womb. I was rather obsessively diligent with researching the developmental stages of the fetus in the womb, and apparently, at fifteen weeks of gestation, the fetus is able to hear. So I started intentionally reading books aloud, particularly novels and fairy tales, partly for personal pleasure but also for the good of my unborn child. I continued reading all types of books out loud consistently every single day up until birth. That was when all the first-time-mom craziness came swarming in, which meant I needed some down time, and I resumed reading at seven weeks postpartum. From then on, I only occasionally missed a day or two of story time with my son. Other than that, I made a habit of reading a little each day and it has yielded exceptional results. At twenty five months old, it was really fascinating to see my son develop a preference for certain types of books. It was especially rewarding when he requested more story time on the days when I didn't initiate the activity. Gradually, the more your child enjoys reading and gets used to the act of reading every day, the less effort you will have to put in to encourage your child to read. I strongly believe that with consistency throughout the years and dedication to recognizing the importance of reading, my son will never lose his curiosity and inquisitive nature that he was born with. He will treat books like companions and make the most of them to become a well-read and knowledgeable person. The reason why cultivating the love for reading is such an important part of raising a bilingual child lies in the love for learning - not for learning any particular language but for general learning in itself.

Principle Three:
Ability to Focus

Cultivate the ability to focus and a love for learning. A person's ability to focus allows them to tune out distractions and zoom in on what truly interests them. Reading, working memory, and abstract thoughts are all aided by our capacity to focus intently on what we're doing, as researched by professors from Göteborg University in Sweden [25]. Researchers at the American Psychological Association agree that children's ability to focus has a direct bearing on how well they learn [26]. You may not realize it, but your child's ability to focus usually increases by 2-3 minutes per year of age. That is, a one-year-old baby can concentrate for 2-3 minutes uninterrupted. A two-year-old can focus for 4-6 minutes. A three-year-old, 6-9 minutes. A four-year-old, 8-12 minutes. Children under the age of five, maximum fifteen minutes. Concentration ability reaches 32-48 minutes by the age of sixteen (which is the length of a school lesson). Of course, the ability to focus is affected by a variety of factors, including noise or surroundings, whether the child is hungry or tired, and how interesting the activity is. Some scientists believe that the standard of 2-3 minutes for each year of a child's age is only an average number, and that two-year-olds can perfectly concentrate for 10-15 minutes given the right circumstances and upbringing. Similarly, a ten-year-old's attention span can be as little as that of a two-year-old if she hadn't been given the right upbringing. If a child's ability to concentrate falls below the above limit, parents should pay closer attention to the child and try to extend the child's ability to concentrate.

This is critical because whether your child has good concentration or not is a prerequisite for his later ability to learn, acquire knowledge, think, and analyze. This includes the abilities required for language learning. Concentration is a natural ability that every child is born with. Our job as parents is merely to preserve and nourish it. Every child is born with a curious mind, but their attention span starts out very short. It lengthens as the child grows. We are in charge of ensuring that this inborn ability matures to its best. There are a lot of things that many parents often do without realizing that they are hindering the child's ability to focus, which will be discussed in great detail later in this book. This ability is actually the foundation for learning in the child's future. Concentration is the foundation for absorbing new knowledge. We, as parents, must be mindful about what we do, what we say, how we say it, and when.

The ability to focus is not much different from the ability to learn, to explore, to better oneself. Very young children have a very short attention span. With time and with the right conditions provided, this attention span will lengthen. As parents, it is our responsibility to create an atmosphere conducive to the development of a child's attention span. Everything your child does throughout the day requires a certain level of concentration, from opening and closing a box or putting together puzzle pieces, to moving an item from one location to another, putting on clothes and shoes, to coloring and helping around the house. Remember that "play is the work of a child" (as famously said by Maria Montessori), so everything that your child does is important. Nothing is meaningless, however small, irrelevant or trivial you may think it is. Unlike us adults, everything a child does helps them learn and discover something new. They acquire new knowledge, gain a new skill, practice an old skill, invent, create, imagine, and understand through doing. So, in order for the child to do all these things to the best of their ability, they need to be able to concentrate.

This third principle is particularly applicable to absorbing languages in everyday life. Learning languages, in particular, requires a high level of concentration because it's not just remembering a list of vocabulary. Learning, or rather acquiring, a language is more than memorizing vocabulary; it's about comprehending the usage and the intrinsic of a foreign language, associating meaning across two or more languages with each other, and connecting verbal, non-verbal, tangible, intangible, visual, and non-visual subjects. It is an art to understand which language can be used to talk to whom, who is able to speak English and who is not. Children have to understand that with those who are not able to speak English, they have to choose a language they can use to communicate with that person. Teaching your child to focus is crucial not just for their academic success (when they may be learning a second language or attending college), but also for their lifelong journey on Earth. As written brilliantly by Ryan Holiday, the author of "Stillness is the key", *it is in those moments of a still and focused mind that our inborn brilliance emerges*. We must learn to quiet the mind even in the midst of noise and chaos to truly excel and not drown.

As with everything in my personal experience, there are no rigid rules per se, but there are certain principles that I strictly adhered to in order to cultivate strong concentration skill for my son. First and foremost, respect your child. As I mentioned earlier, everything that your child does is important. It might not seem important or big to you, but it is important. Respect your child's needs and reasons. When your child is in the middle of a certain activity, whatever it may be, as long as it's safe, then respect your child's personal space. Respect their boundaries. Make sure that they are given time and space to do their own exploration without you hovering above their heads and telling them what something is, how to use it, and what to do with it. Let your child use their creative mind to develop their own skills and their own version of life.

Respect also applies to situations where you have a preconception of time in the duration of things and sequence of events, but your child doesn't. For example, when you are at the park, you know that you had planned to go there for an hour before having to leave to run an errand. You can look at your watch and know that it's almost time to go, but your child doesn't know that. Instead of forcefully making them leave the playground, you need to rise above this common parenting and respect your child's understanding of the world. It is not difficult to give them some form of advance warning, give them information on what to expect. Very young children who don't yet have an understanding of time can't tell what five or thirty minutes means. You might want to visualize time for them. For example, "How about you slide two more times and then it's time to go home" or "It's almost time to go home. Are you done with the slide? Do you want to go on the swing before we head home?" Simple and mindfully curated sentences like this will show your child that you respect them, and it will essentially prevent tantrums because children thrive when they know what to expect. Choose your own battles and be more mindful about your child's view of the world. By giving them these little pieces of information, you help them navigate their own existence panic-free.

To ensure that your child has the best possible environment for cultivating their own ability to focus, you need to prepare your home and any other environments that your child might be in. Often, we see parents buy a big basket or box for toys and dump all the toys in it without any particular order. What the child will do every single time they want to play with a toy is dump everything out, everywhere. Gradually, that toy box becomes their representation of playtime: messy and chaotic. At the end of the day, everything gets put back into that big box. Repeat. Not only does the notion of a "toy box dump" give a lot of us an instant migraine, but it also does not serve our children in any positive way. All the toys are mixed up, missing, broken, nowhere to be found, and overwhelming. Imagine wanting to play with puzzles but in order to do that you must dig through a massive toy box to find all the pieces, which might not all be there. By the time you've done the digging, would you still want to do the puzzle? Instead of falling into the toy box trap, you can be mindful about the presentation of toys to your child. Limit the number of toys to a certain number (say, fifteen) so that your child is not overwhelmed with a massive amount of toys that sometimes they don't even know what to do with. Make sure that wherever the toys are designated to be in your home, they are within your child's reach. You might want to invest in a special shelf or you might just use the lowest two or three shelves from your own existing shelves. Safety first, which means that whatever is within reach of your child should be childproof and should be safe to access.

Children are creatures of habit and order. There is a great benefit in remembering that for your child, "everything has its place." What I found that has worked wonders in our home is that every set of toys should have a box or container designated for it. Avoid mixing different sets of toys because that creates confusion and disorder for your child. It disrupts the natural ability to put things where they belong, which your child is inherently born with. If a set of close-ended toys (like puzzles) is missing a piece, make sure that the whole set is removed from your child's toy area. Everything that your child is presented with on a reachable level should be playable. In the case of open-ended toys (like building blocks), it's fine if a piece is missing because there are other ways to play with it. If the toy is broken, remove it.

I am aware that this is all significantly more demanding for the parent than the traditionally used "toy box dump" method, but the benefits outweigh the trouble by miles, not just now, but in the long term as well. Apart from toys, this sense of focus and keeping order also applies to daily activities. We are all too guilty of procrastination every now and then, if not all the time. But children do as we do, not as we say. You can't expect your child to keep things in order if you set an example by constantly putting things off to do later. You, as an adult, have a longer attention span. You can keep to-do lists. You can strategically plan your day. You can make plans, both immediate, short term, and long term. Your child doesn't have the cognitive ability to do that. So, if something needs to be done, like cleaning up after eating or throwing something in the trash can, then you need to set an example and do it right away instead of waiting to do it when you get up from the sofa. If your child opens a bag of sweets and the packaging needs to be thrown away into the trash can, you have to model that action right away for your child. Gradually, you won't have to actually get up, but your child will do it themselves because they know that is the right sequence of events. Things need to be put where they belong, which includes trash. If you spill something, whether liquid or solid, you should, particularly when your child is watching, clean it up right away instead of putting it off until it's convenient. For your child, that doesn't make sense. If you want to create a habit of tidiness, independence, order, and the ability to concentrate on tasks for your child, then you need to start by modelling the completed sequence of events right away without interruption or delay.

I actually learned this from my own experience. I found that it has great benefits, not just for the behavior of my child, but also for myself. I find that I am becoming a better person because I am trying to model being a good and responsible person for my child. What better goal to set for yourself than to be admired by your child? Self-actualization is definitely an added bonus of respectful parenting.

Another way to nurture your child's ability to concentrate is to include the element of human interaction, respectfully, fiercely, and gently. It is essential that parents directly interact and converse with their children frequently during the day and every day. There is a difference between absent human interaction and present human interaction. Absent human interaction is when the parent is present, but they are really thinking about something else, like work, marriage, or some other adult problems. Maybe they are just simply thinking about something more interesting to them than their kid's play. As a result, whenever the child talks to the parent, the parent tends to respond in an absentminded manner by saying things like "Oh yeah," "That's really interesting," or "Oh really! That's great". But present human interaction is much, much more than that. It requires the parent's understanding that nothing their child says is trivial. They also understand the reality that even though our children are small, their minds and their feelings are huge. I dare to presume that you are a *present parent*, judging by your decision to buy and read this book.

Parents should be fully present in the eyes of their children as much as possible. Pay attention to what your child is telling you. Wait for them to finish. Do not interfere. Do not lead. Give them a chance and space to fully express themselves, to explain things to you, to relay their own version of their stories. Then be mindful about asking about their feelings. "How did that make you feel?", "What else happened?", "What did you like about it?", "What did you dislike about it?" Young children are naturally impulsive creatures; their behaviour is essentially guided by emotions and feelings. It is very important to pay attention to their feelings through whatever story they are telling you.

You can upgrade the level of present human interaction by adding certain elements of learning. For example, your child is telling you about a recent walk where they saw some leaves, flowers, and trees, maybe a bee or a butterfly, too. You might want to upgrade the level of that conversation by asking about the color of the butterfly or the size of the flowers. Ask about the weather or whether the leaves were green or brown, fresh or dry. Keep extending the story mindfully. Pay full attention to every word your child says and even repeat the words if your child seems encouraged by the fact that you understand everything they say.

Your attention is the biggest encouragement for your child.

Pay attention to your child's communication and then extend that communication by adding different layers of interest whilst maintaining the age appropriateness of the questions you ask. Age appropriateness includes not asking questions that are too tricky or too difficult. Avoid asking any questions that you know will be too challenging for your child - it is not funny, in contrast to what many people seem to think. Leading your child to say/repeat something "funny" that they do not understand merely for the sake of your own amusement is not beneficial to your child's development.

Children are encouraged and motivated when they can do something, answer questions, or simply feel that they are being heard. Your child is capable of solving problems, such as how to make a tower taller using different shaped blocks, while knowing that you are nearby if they need help. This gives your child an "I can do it" attitude towards even more difficult tasks in the future. Similarly, they are discouraged when they can't answer a question or feel they don't know something. A commonly accepted custom is that it is a good idea to let your child win even when they actually lost in a game, but equally important it is to let your child lose (without mocking) and learn to accept defeat. This will help them understand that losing as well as winning is a normal part of life and help them learn to process and move on instead of being majorly upset about it. One way to cultivate this reaction is by demonstrating how you handle defeat. You should remain calm and treat defeat or victory as a normal part of the game. You could help by saying, "I lost this time. Let's try again."

> *There was a lovely instance when my son pleasantly surprised me. We were playing basketball in his toy room when I threw the ball and missed the hoop. I said, "Oh no, I missed!" with a somewhat sad facial expression. What my three-year-old responded to that almost brought tears to my eyes. He said, "That's okay mummy. Let's do it again." They really do learn all the wonderful things that we teach them!*

Remember never to mock your child about losing because that is what sparks resentment and anger in the long-term whenever your child loses in a game or competition in the future. Jean Piaget once famously wrote: "Knowledge arises neither from objects nor the child, but from interactions between the child and those objects," which can be applied to both objects and situations.

Bonus Principle:
What is the parents speak the second language only a little or not at all?

You might say, "That's all great in principle - but what about a situation where the parents don't speak a foreign language well enough to be using it *frequently, constantly,* and *repetitively*?" Or perhaps neither parent can speak a second language *at all*? If this is the case, then first of all, well done to you. You realise the importance of your child speaking multiple languages, even though you don't. This is the most important first step. When the parents realize how important bilingualism is, it will help them have strength, determination, and patience to persevere through the process, especially when the hard bumps come along. It is possible to raise your children to be somewhat bilingual, even if you don't speak more than one language yourself. Firstly, try not to teach your child a "broken" version of the secondary language. More often than not, I see situations where the parents only speak Vietnamese, but they want their child to speak both Vietnamese and English. It is tempting for these parents to try to learn words and sentences in English and immediately teach these words to their children. I would not recommend that you do this. If you don't use the foreign language correctly and go on to teach your child the wrong way to use that language, then instead of setting a solid foundation for bilingualism, you are unintentionally creating language problems down the line for your child. When they grow up, or hear other kids around them speak English, and they find out that what they know is wrong, they will eventually self-correct and reverse the "broken" version of the language, but depending on the child, they might also lose confidence in themselves and stop enjoying learning the language altogether.

Instead, try to expose your child to environments and people who actually use English properly. Many people might disagree with me on this, but one of the easiest tools to help expose your child to proper usage of English is TV. Before you bash me for recommending screen time to young children, hear me out. I'm not saying you should sit your child in front of the TV for hours on end with the excuse of language learning. No, boundaries, discipline, and mindfulness are key. You should be closely monitoring the channels and shows your child is allowed to watch. You should carefully select the content that you expose your children to. Some parents believe that children under two years of age should not have any screen time at all. I disagree. My son has learnt a great deal from watching channels on YouTube like Little Baby Bum and Cocomelon. From age two onwards, he really enjoyed Teletubbies and Peppa Pig. Now that he is three, he really enjoys more advanced, educational shows like Blippi and Numberblocks, as well as cartoon shows with storyplots like Paw Patrol and various superhero shows such as Batman and Spiderman. Not only is it helping with language learning as he repeats almost every word he hears, but also, he gains a visual knowledge of the world. When we see similar things outdoors, at the zoo, in the park, or in any other area of our lives, he can very quickly relate to the visual knowledge that he had seen on TV. My role then is to spot those things and say their names in English and Vietnamese; the rest of the learning is done by my toddler.

To avoid the trap of mindless TV addiction, you should not let your child submerge himself in TV shows by letting him become a couch potato while you try to tick off your to-do lists and chores around the house. Try to see the TV as an entertainer for your child (that's the way I see it anyway). Be present when your child is watching TV, sing with your child, interact, show emotions whenever you see something surprising, funny, or scary. Not only will this facilitate positive associations and language learning for your child, but it will also increase your bond and help you stay aware of all the digital content your child is consuming.

A variation of learning languages through screen time is *unconscious listening.* This means that your child absorbs a second language through their auditory senses without consciously realizing it. Invest in an audio player without a screen (not your smartphone). I frequently upload and switch around different audio files, such as educational English songs, nursery rhymes, and age-appropriate short stories. The audio can be played in the background during your child's independent play or quiet time. Your child's hand and eye coordination are then focused on his current toy or activity, as he is not actively speaking, which is a window of opportunity for unconscious listening. With time, your child will start to repeat the phrases he hears. Obviously, this is a slower process than actual daily interactions in a foreign language because your child doesn't have a physical representation of what the words mean. However, a balanced combination of both selective screen time and unconscious listening will help your child gradually grasp the meaning of words and expressions. You could accelerate this process by combining audio files with children's books. Many picture books for children in English are accompanied by an audio file. It would be a good idea to invest in those picture books and the audio files because if you don't know how to read English properly, you can sit your child on your lap, play the audio while flipping through the book, showing emotions and pointing at things as you hear them from the audio player. That way, you will help your child visualize the meaning of the words that they are hearing.

Another idea for parents who don't speak foreign languages but want their children to speak foreign languages is *attending playgroups*. A child develops their language skills significantly more quickly when they are surrounded by children around their own age. It's a good idea to expose your child to playgroups where children and adults are able to speak more than one language. If you are based in Vietnam, then recently there's been an increase in the popularity of indoor playground cafes. From my own experience, the staff at the smaller-scale ones often speak English to the children. Moreover, such indoor playground cafes have become a popular location for play dates of mixed-race families where one or both parents are of non-Vietnamese origin. As parents and children are often of mixed nationalities, your child will be exposed to real-life bilingualism through play and conversation.

Above are just a few things that parents who only speak one language can do to help increase their child's exposure to the secondary language as frequently, repetitively, and constantly as possible. The above, of course, omits the mention of pre-school selection. What we want to focus on here is language education within the home rather than at school with teachers. We focus on how children can learn to speak two languages even before they start school. Of course, it is always a good idea for the parents to take language classes themselves so that they can learn and grow in terms of language development with the child. This is quite a beneficial way to approach things because you essentially kill two birds with one stone. Not only will you gain a new language yourself, but you will also give your child the priceless gift of bilingualism for life.

There is also the *power of positive affirmations* and the reality that your children will become what you tell them. If you believe in them, praise them, let them know what they are great at. You have the responsibility to make them believe in themselves and to make them think that they are capable of doing great things, including speaking not one, but two, maybe three or more languages. I can't even put a number on how many parents I know who repeatedly tell their children that they are "troublemakers", "badly performing students", or "rebels" that always oppose their parents. Kids often become the words that are spoken about them. This point leads to the next chapter about mindful and respectful parenting being the underlying groundwork for successful multilingual parenting.

6

UNDERLYING GROUNDWORK FOR MULTILINGUAL PARENTING

Mindfulness: Observant and Present

I am sure you will have heard this at one point or another. When someone tells you "Don't think of a pink elephant", you think of a pink elephant. When someone keeps describing their son as a "troublemaker", he will surely prove you right and in fact be (or become) a troublemaker. If you want your child to speak a foreign language, make them believe that they can do it. Instead of stating to your child that English is difficult and overpraising your child for simply muttering one or two English words, make them believe that acquiring English and Vietnamese is both fun and enjoyable. You tell them that they are good listeners and good learners. Quit saying "No, you're wrong." Let us revisit an instance when my son was learning about animals. We have these little animal figurines—a whole box full of them—and very often we just sit down on the floor and learn animal names and sounds. There were times when my son was obsessed with turtles, other times he was obsessed with wolves, or horses, and so on. One time, I showed him an eagle and asked him what it was in English. I knew that he knew the answer, but he wasn't answering me because his mind was preoccupied with the turtle. He kept saying "turtle, turtle". Instead of saying "No, you're wrong," which he obviously was because I asked him about an eagle and he kept saying turtle, I redirected my own attention and following his lead by saying "Oh, is that a turtle?" "Wow, can you act like a turtle?" The point was to try to *elaborate* on his interests, to *follow his lead*, instead of saying that he is wrong because he didn't do what I was asking of him. Not only did this little instance give him a positive association with learning about animals in English, but it also increased the quality and effectiveness of the actual learning time. If he does not want to show interest in "eagles", then no matter how many times I teach him the name of an eagle and how an eagle acts, he will not be receptive.

A mindful parent must be observant, not forceful.

Follow your child's lead because that's the best way they learn. Children are naturally curious learners. They learn very well and very fast, but they learn on their own terms. You can't force a two-year-old to sit still in one chair for 20-30 minutes at a time to listen while you recite the names of animals. By nature, it simply doesn't work that way. Sometimes, your toddler is going to be running around the house with his arms spread wide, pretending to be a butterfly. Sometimes, he is going to be crawling around the house pretending to be a snake while hissing like a snake. Sometimes, he will sit still for fifteen minutes staring at nothing, randomly say the names of different animals. That's when he's learning! Your role is to be observant and do what works best for your child. Not for *you*, but for *your child*.

This attitude equally applies to the selection of books,

choice of games, types of TV shows, list of audio files, songs, poems, and stories that you choose to expose your child to. They will best learn about something they are interested in. They do not have the cognitive capability to force themselves to learn something that they don't enjoy. We, as adults, have been through much more in life, and sometimes we understand that it is essential to learn, study, or endure something that we don't really enjoy. But for very young kids, it doesn't work that way. *If they don't want it, they don't want it.* And that's actually the reason for many tantrums, especially the uncontrollable and inconsolable ones. Behavioral outbursts happen because of the discrepancy between *our* understanding of the world and *their* understanding of the world. We often expect things from them that they are not capable of comprehending. We need to be more observant of our children. We need to be more mindful of their development and what they can understand, or even mentally handle, at different phases of their lives.

Okay, that's all great - you might say. But what about when your child throws a tantrum that is by definition unreasonable and unallowable, like when it's freezing cold outside, and your child simply refuses to put on a coat or shoes? How do you follow the child's lead then? How do you practice mindful parenting then? One thing about very young children is that their sense of logic and consequences hasn't fully developed, so they simply don't want to put a coat on because they don't want to. That's it! They don't tend to think beyond that. They don't think that "Because it is cold outside, if I go out without a coat, I might freeze and get ill." No, they don't think that far ahead. In their minds, they don't want to put a coat on right then, full stop. No reason. That might change in the next two seconds. Or it might not. If we keep forcing it, then the child goes into tantrum mode, which essentially means resisting whatever is asked of them then and there. If they do this often enough, then it will become a habit.

How do we prevent repeated occurrences of tantrums? We often hear all the parenting books advise us to "choose our battles", especially when we are knee-deep into the phase of toddlerhood. I am all for "you do you" and I am well aware that no two parenting journeys look alike. But here is the way I normally choose my battles. If my son does not want to put on a coat or shoes, I take him outside in a short-sleeved shirt or bare-feet and let him decide if it's cold. I will tell him that my coat is keeping me warm, so I don't feel cold. "Do you feel cold? Do you think that your body might need a coat to keep you warm?" - I will ask him. Executed gently and positively enough, this strategy might just make your child think that they need a coat. He'll then "make a decision" *on his own* to put on a coat or shoes. Mission accomplished! Keep in mind that your toddler is still a human being with his own mind and not a robot with dependable programming, so don't expect it to work all the time. Some days you'll be stuck in the car with a fussy kid, some days your kid will be wearing shorts in the dead of winter. And that's okay.

Sometime around last June, way before Halloween, my son - around twenty months old at the time - suddenly became overly obsessed with all things Halloween. From zombies to vampires, skeletons, ghosts, monsters, pumpkins, and Jack O'Lanterns. He had watched some children's videos about Halloween on YouTube and they instantly grabbed his attention. From then on, he kept asking for "skeleton" on TV, which meant Halloween. (Please note that this was in June.) Gradually, he had developed his vocabulary for all things related to Halloween. By the time Halloween actually came (around five months later), luckily he was not bored of Halloween yet. He was rather extremely fascinated because he could see around him everything that he already knew, like pumpkins, ghosts, zombies, haunted houses. He was only nineteen to twenty months old when the Halloween obsession started. If I had decided that it was not Halloween time, therefore no point in learning about Halloween just yet, then I would have missed out on the opportunity to help my son develop his vocabulary, as well as help myself develop his understanding of the topic. Moreover, because of those few months of Halloween obsession, the result is that he's not afraid of the dark or so-called monsters. When he sees a skeleton, he points to it with joy. When he sees a mummy or zombie picture, he just makes funny gestures and acts like a zombie to jokingly scare us (mummy and daddy).

I can see that following my son's lead back then has had a far greater meaning than the mere introduction of the Halloween festival. It has had immense benefits for his imagination, creativity, and curiosity. In a couple of years, when most kids are afraid of silly things because adults told them so, my son will be willing to explore new things with joy and excitement. Because he's not afraid, he will freely explore the world to the fullest of his cognitive capacity, which I think is one of the benefits that we would not have been able to foresee before the whole experience happened. My takeaway message from this was that so long as what grabs his interest is not ethically toxic, age-inappropriate, violently dangerous, or falls too far out of the cultural norms, then I think there is no reason not to follow the child's lead fully. The benefits are just widely and wonderfully unexpected.

As I was drafting this section of the manuscript, we were one month away from Christmas. But low and behold, as much of a Christmas addict as I've been my entire life, my son didn't really show any particular interest in Christmas-related things, except that

Santa Claus says, "Ho Ho Ho". When he saw a Christmas tree in our apartment entrance hall, he was interested. But his interest was more in the shiny ornaments than the Christmas tree itself. When I sang "Rudolph the red nosed reindeer" to him, he found it funny because he liked animals in general but didn't particularly pursue this interest any further. So, as sad as it made me (because I am obsessed with Christmas), I've got to respect my child's interests and his natural desire to learn, and let Christmas go – for now. "Most children like receiving presents, and I am sure that my son will be very happy when he opens his presents on Christmas Day. But if he is not too keen on the advent period, then I am in no position to force it on him" – I kept telling myself. To be honest, he was still more interested in skeletons and pumpkins than reindeer and Christmas trees. This was my way of showing that I am a respectful and mindful parent.

Without holding any presumptions about a few years down the line, when my son starts school, my firm belief and expectation is that I don't want my son to be *forcefully learning*. The current education system in the country where I live is rather outdated. Even though I am a university lecturer and I try my best to make my classes as innovative and student-centered as possible, my son will still have to go through primary, secondary, and tertiary education before he gets to university. Professionally, I am not part of the national primary education system; but at home, I am my son's primary and life-long educator. I intend to respectfully and reasonably, with the appropriate balance, create the most student-centered environment and learning experience for my son possible. All the forced endless hours of homework or non-interactive class time just wears our children out, then gradually, perhaps by second grade, they realize that learning is not fun. The outdated education system does not allow room for a much-needed balance between study and play, or rather the incorporation of study into play. I can't repeat this enough: "Play is the work of a child" as famously said by Maria Montessori. Children can't sit in the classroom for hours on end. They need time and space to develop their social skills, practice interactions, spend quality time with their families, and learn about cultural aspects of life.

I come across so many children who suffer and dread the idea of school as early as the first grade, which pains me on so many levels. It's not just my opinion, but it is widely proven that learning in young children is significantly accelerated when the child has fun. Young children learn best through doing, touching, and moving around, rather than repetitive dictations, textbook recitations, or endlessly watching teachers write things on chalkboards. They are not receptive to boring PowerPoint slides. I remember my own time in primary school in Poland. The most vivid memories of my education were spent outdoors, picking dry leaves and learning about different types of trees. Even when we stayed inside the classroom, there were no designated desks and chairs for each student. Instead, we were usually all on the floor on a special carpet with streets, roads, buildings, and general infrastructure printed on it as we learned about traffic, different types of buildings, hospitals, schools, and stores. Even math lessons were brought to life by the most amazing teachers. We didn't sit and write in our notebooks endlessly. We would use different tools that we could tangibly hold in our hands to perform fractions, multiplications, or geometry. I remember everything was done in a fun way. Looking from an administrative point of view, none of it was particularly difficult to organize or replicate. It then brings me to our current education system. Prolongment of an outdated education system comes at a cost of hindered future development of the economy. All our future leaders are essentially in primary schools now. Here is the obvious question: *How to make our future better?*. And here is the obvious answer: *Educate our children better!*

Even dating back to 1992, K. Ann Renninger, a professor at Swarthmore College, wrote in her book chapter [27] that "most of the time, we are reasonably accurate if we assume that student learning is influenced by interest", which she defined as things that evoke prolonged child attention and engagement. She, however, did not have an answer back then as to why this was the case. Active learning, which is the direct and immediate experience of things, people, ideas, and events, is a requirement for cognitive development. Simply put, young children learn concepts, form ideas, and make their own symbols or abstractions by doing things on their own, like moving, listening, looking, touching, and manipulating. When this kind of activity is done in a social setting where an alert and sensitive adult is a participant-observer, the child can have experiences that are interesting on their own and that may lead to contradictory conclusions and a reorganization of how the child sees the world. Understanding the world is a slow, gradual process in which children attempt to incorporate brand new observations into what they already know or believe they know about reality. As a result, children often reach various conclusions, some of which may be incorrect in the eyes of an adult. When adults communicate with children, they should understand that this kind of thinking is part of the active learning process and accept children's reasoning that differs from their own. Children's thinking will eventually match that of adults, or even exceed it.

Cognitive developmentalists claim that learning is a process in which a child acts on and interacts with the world around him or her to build up a more complex idea of what reality is.

Through experience, a child develops incomplete ideas that can lead to contradictory conclusions. The process of figuring out how to solve these contradictions makes the child's thinking and learning more complex. For example, a child notices that most of the balls he has seen are round and bouncy. He says to himself, "My Play-Doh ball is round. It will bounce." He learns that the Play-Doh ball is round, but when he bounces it, it sticks to the floor. He realizes that he needs a new way of thinking to make sense of his old conclusions and new observations: "That ball outside bounces, but this Play-Doh ball doesn't bounce." Even though he has changed his view of reality in response to new information, his new explanation is still not complete. This is because developmental change occurs slowly, in small increments, and is a self-evolving and self-correcting process. A child usually needs to try out a new idea many times before they understand it.

John Flavel, a developmental psychologist, said in 1963 [28] that children can only take in parts of reality that their minds can handle without having to change too drastically. The world around them can only be understood if they actively engage with it. Children learn more about the world as they do things to try out ideas or find answers to questions. When a young child reaches for a ball, for example, he or she is trying to answer an internal question such as, "I wonder what this thing does." By acting (grabbing, tasting, chewing, dropping, pushing, and rolling) and then thinking about these actions, the child starts to answer the question and build their own understanding of what balls do. In other words, a child thinks and understands more as a result of what he or she *does* and how he or she *thinks* about it. So, *action* on its own is not enough to learn, it must be combined with *reflection*. Active learning is both the physical act of interacting with things to see what happens and the mental act of trying to figure out what happened and how it fits into their prior knowledge and a bigger understanding of the world.

Most of my education was in Poland and England, but I also had a few years of studying in Vietnam, and what I remember from my one year of primary education in Vietnam is having to carry a five-kilo backpack to school every single day. If one day I forgot a certain notebook or textbook, I would be "punished" by the teacher. The punishment was usually in the form of standing in the corner of the class for the entire lesson. Sometimes, in order to avoid being forced to sit and study all day with both of my arms on the desk looking straight at the chalkboard and reciting things that the teacher said, I would deliberately leave a book or a notebook at home so that I could stand in the corner and have a different view of the class that day. Even standing in silence alone was more fun for me (and many of my friends) than "studying".

It is so vividly clear in my mind that the difference between my two experiences of primary education, one in Poland and one in Vietnam, was sadly but shockingly large. This gives me an incredible motivation to make a change, however small, so that my son does not have to suffer through the inadequate and outdated primary education system. Ask yourself today, are you satisfied with the way your child is learning at school? If so, good for you. If not, take a stand and make a change. We, parents, are both the beneficiaries and customers of schools, so we should have the greatest power after all.

A young child has a mind of their own. You, as a parent, understand them the most. You must be mindful and observant of your child's mind and thoughts. Sometimes adults keep asking toddlers a lot of things, usually quizzing them about vocabulary or objects around the house or some new sentence they have learned to say. But you will notice that a lot of the time you have to repeat your child's name or get their attention several times before they react. That's not because they are stubborn, ignorant, or purposely not paying attention to you. That is because most of the time, they are focused on something else. Maybe they are looking at their own shadow in a wardrobe that has a shiny coat of paint. Maybe they are observing the hands of the clock moving. Maybe they are trying to listen to some sounds that you are not even noticing. When you call your child, try not to call more than twice. When you are nearby, gently say their name, or gently nudge them. If they don't react, then you need to observe from their perspective and try to see what they might be thinking about, feeling, or noticing at that very moment. Remember that if you get it right and you gently say: "the clock is ticking, isn't it?" or "the clock has numbers on it, doesn't it?" then you hit the jackpot and get a faster reaction as well as their full attention. The other day, my son saw some birds flying outside our balcony, and he stood in the middle of our living room looking outwards at quite a distance. What I saw was him suddenly just standing frozen in the living room. Instead of interrupting by asking "what are you doing?". I took three seconds to observe and follow his gaze. I saw two birds in the sky, and I remained quiet. I let the situation pass, and then when he moved his eyes, which meant to me that his cycle of attention on the birds was finished, I asked him, "Did you see two birds in the sky?". He was very happy that I noticed it too, and he nodded very cheerfully. He started talking about how birds fly and flapped his arms, pretending he was a bird. Tiny situations like that bear huge significance in our household. Although tiny, they occur regularly and frequently. Build up your child's sense of trust, sense of confidence, positivity, and eagerness to learn. Your reward will be a respectful and well-rounded adult, well set up for success in life.

Respectfulness: Fierce but Gentle

Being a young parent can be hard. Many parenting programs and books focus on teaching parenting skills such as feeding, sleep training, and must-have baby gear instead of creating a strong relationship (commonly referred to as "bonding") between the parent and child from the very first days. In the Journal of Child and Family Studies, Dr Amanda Richardson, Dr Johnny Lo, and Dr Therese O'Sullivan of Edith Cowan University, together with Dr Lynn Priddis of the University of Western Australia [29], looked into whether the Respectful Parenting Approach, which is based on building relationships between parents and children through observation and respect, makes parents of babies and toddlers feel less stressed and more confident. The results from this quasi-experimental study confirmed that it does.

I suppose the first and foremost foundation for parenting is *trust* from your children. To gain their trust, you must trust them. From my extensive research and years of obsession (to say the least) over what is the best way to do "the parenting" thing, I learned that respecting your children and treating them like actual people is probably the most effective way to gain their trust. They need to trust you in order to communicate with you. Once you can communicate with your children, that is "an open gate" for you to teach them anything you want. You can make sure that they grow up to be good people, confident in themselves, and believe they can learn and do whatever they desire. That is a long-term view, but for now, let's go back to the initial stage of parenting, the early years.

What is "respectful parenting"? And what are the biggest misconceptions about it? There are terms that are used interchangeably with *respectful parenting*, such as "positive parenting", "attachment parenting", among others. Essentially, they mean the same thing. They mean that you treat your children like actual people, without imposing that you are the controlling one. Most "traditional" parents insist they have the right to do whatever they want, their way; they are the parents, so their children must listen to them and do what they say. I hate to break it to them, but that is not *it*. *Respectful parenting* means giving your child the right to decide for themselves what they want to do, how they want to feel, how they see things, how they conduct themselves, and how they behave. Respectful parenting should be distinguished from "permissive parenting" which is letting your child be borderless and wild without giving them any guidance or tools. Respectful parenting should also be distinguished from "controlling parenting" which is imposing rules your children must obey on a constant basis. Many people mistakenly believe that respectful parenting is permissive parenting, letting your child do whatever they please, whenever they please. But that is so far from the truth.

There is a middle ground between
permissive parenting and controlling parenting.
And on this "ground", the overarching aura is
love, empathy, and respect.

The underlying mindset that we have got to adopt is that our children are not just robots for us to train; they are actual human beings with their own minds, their own feelings, and their own logic. They can also form opinions, their own view of the world, and preferences too, however young. We have got to treat them like actual human beings. What that means is that we guide them and provide them with the tools to become respectful and empathetic adults. They need to understand that the essence of being a good person is to respect one another instead of doing whatever it takes to make others obey. I bet you have come across or at least heard of bosses in management positions that portray positive, empathetic, and understanding characteristics versus bosses who are controlling and oblivious to anyone's feelings so long as the work is done, and the profits are maximized. Maybe you yourself have such a boss, or maybe you are such a boss, but even from the outside, I bet you can tell the difference in the work quality and productivity under these two different types of management styles. Eventually, the effects of such management will seep into employees' personalities and work cultures.

When your child is a very young baby, they will communicate with you through cries and cues. You learn to understand those with the passage of time. No matter how young, they can show what they are dissatisfied with, what is irritating them emotionally, or making them uncomfortable physically. They expect you to react and to make them comfortable again. When they are very small, we usually tend to their every need. We tend to make them feel comfortable right away, because otherwise they would be crying endlessly. Their crying is often seen as a so-called inconvenience, especially in public places. Being perfectly honest, my baby used to cry a lot at first, but it never seemed like an inconvenience to me because I understood that crying was his way of communicating with me. Without rushing to make sure that he stopped crying by distracting him, my focus was on finding out the root cause and making him feel better.

To ensure that the bond between parent and child is wholly unconditional, do not challenge the baby's trust in mum. One of my biggest principles when I had my son was to always be his safe haven, to always be the place where he can turn to unconditionally, even when I am upset with him. To achieve that goal, there is no other way than to parent in a fully respectful and mindful way. Be observant, present, gentle but also fierce.

You might say: "Ok, a young baby is easy to comfort, but what about toddlers?" We all hear about the terrible twos, terrible threes, and endless tantrums, which funnily seem to surface at the most inconvenient times, like at the supermarket, at a family gathering, at a wedding, maybe a funeral, or a meeting. How do you then respectfully and consensually give your child the freedom to make his own opinions and choices while he is in a full-blown cry over literally nothing? Well, trust me, I've got a toddler who was in the thick of his terrible twos and moved on to the terrible threes, so I've got quite a handful of such experiences. I would have to say, though, as often as he can have a tantrum and a meltdown at home, I have only had to deal with his tantrum in a public place twice (which I share in the next paragraph). That is not because he is such a good kid and always does what I tell him. That is because he has unconditional trust in his parents, and he knows that his feelings are never invalidated. He knows he can always turn to us and tell us what is bothering him or what he wants, and we will react appropriately to make sure that his needs are met to the most acceptable level. This required us to consciously and mindfully change ourselves from the moment our son was born. These changes were not just in relation to becoming new parents, but rather becoming better people. Children tend to do what you do, not what you say, so we started making small but consistent changes at every turn, to make sure our son had adequate role models at home and in life.

The first time that I had to remove him from a public situation due to a meltdown was in a shopping mall. We were about to leave a supermarket. A lot of people stood in line at the checkout. Our son did not want to leave because he wanted to go back to the toy section and look at some toys. The problem wasn't that he wanted us to buy him some toys. The problem was just that he wasn't finished looking at those toys, even though he had been doing it for about half an hour already. At the time, he was obsessed with eggs—surprise eggs—and conveniently, there were a lot of those eggs in the toy section. He just wanted to stay there and look at those eggs, maybe touch them. But life goes on, and we really had to leave. After successfully removing him from the toy section, we proceeded to walk around in hopes of taking his mind off the eggs for long enough to leave. Then we reached the checkout. As we did so, he realized that we were leaving, so he went into a full-blown mode of inconsolable crying in a matter of seconds. He began shouting and screaming, and everybody turned to look at us. I knew at that point that there was no reasoning with him nor talking to him, so I gently but firmly lifted him up, held him tight in my arms as if I was holding him, but my grasp was very firm so that he couldn't escape. It felt like holding a gorilla having a seizure as I calmly walked away without saying anything to him, and my husband stayed behind to pay for the rest of our groceries. Everybody was looking at us because my son was screaming like a monster. And I wasn't doing anything to comfort him other than holding him firmly (but calmly) in absolute silence. But I understood that he had some big emotions in his little body, and it wasn't an option for us to continue staying at the toy section. As soon as we left the shopping mall, he stopped crying. He just looked around, saw a butterfly, and proceeded to happily chase that butterfly, as if nothing out of the ordinary ever happened. That was when I realized that it was really no big deal unless I made it a big deal.

The second situation of a public tantrum credited to my toddler that I experienced was at a playground where many children were playing. They were of different age ranges, and my son was probably among the youngest. He really liked a scooter that one of the other kids had. He didn't own a scooter, as he was only around a year and a half then. I didn't think he was ready for a scooter, so I simply hadn't bought him one. At the playground, he saw this girl who was probably a couple of years older than him, and she was just scooting away on her little scooter. It looked fun. Obviously, the scooter wasn't his, nor was it a public toy, but he wanted to play with it just as he would with any of the other public toys on the playground. When I told him that he couldn't play with that scooter because it belonged to someone else, he went into a hysterical cry. At first, I thought it would be a good idea to gently talk to him and explain that the scooter wasn't ours, and if he wanted to continue playing at the playground, he needed to move on and play with another toy. The scooter was not a public toy, it belonged to that girl, and only that girl could play with it (she did not agree to let my son borrow it). He was a bit too small for that scooter anyway. He stopped crying and calmly looked at me while still glancing over at the scooter. But then, he went back into hysteria again. Because gently talking and reasoning with him didn't work, the only choice I had was to gently but firmly remove him from the situation. It was very important to maintain calm and respectful but also firmly and gently get hold of him and remove him from that situation without saying anything further.

In neither of these situations did I shout, scold, or hit my son because I understood that he wasn't showcasing those tantrums on purpose. It was just the way that his feelings evolved, and he didn't know how to deal with those feelings just yet. So, my role was not to punish him for not doing something that he didn't know how to do. My role was to give him space to learn how to behave in such situations. But sometimes staying in the situation would do more harm than good because he had already entered the "unreasonable" and "inconsolable'' phase. The way I usually think about it is simply "*abort the mission, try again next time*". It doesn't mean that I failed nor that I lost any "mum" points. It doesn't mean that I am a bad parent nor that I have a bad kid. None of those things are true. It's just life, and that's the way children grow and become adults - through learning from experiences.

Our children's bodies are not born fully grown; they have to start from a place where they can't even roll over or lift their heads; then they will crawl; then sit; then stand; then walk; then run; then jump. This is the same way their minds need to develop. Their minds need to grow from an inability to process feelings, thoughts, and information gradually to a place where they can properly and respectfully deal with everything that comes their way. Just like not everyone will physically become a supermodel, not everyone will become a respectful and empathetic human being. It really comes down to the way people are raised as very young children.

The next thing that might help respectful parenting work smoothly is to allow your child *choices.* A child's sense of logic is not yet developed in the very early years, which means that their demands and requests often seem unreasonable or illogical to adults. In order to minimize the unreasonable and illogical situations to the absolute minimum, you can try giving your child choices. This has to be done rather skillfully and mindfully. I say this not in the sense that you need to manipulate your child, but rather when your child is fighting bath time, one way to deal with this situation might be to give your child choices by asking, "Do you want the shower or the bathtub?" Even though this seems like the simplest way of offering choices, it often won't work because they are smart enough to realize the common essence of the options you've given is still taking a bath. However, you can tweak it slightly by saying, "Now we are going into the bath. Do you want to take the yellow duck or the blue elephant with you into the bath?". This redirects your child's attention from the fact that they must take a bath to the fact that they will be able to play in the bath. Now they are faced with the choice of one among two toys.

Let me give you another example of a situation where giving choices might solve your struggle. For example, while going to the supermarket often sounds like fun to children, there are moments when your child wants to keep doing something like playing with blocks instead of going to the supermarket for groceries. But sometimes, you simply cannot delay your grocery trip any longer for various reasons that life usually hits you with. How do you get your child to go to the supermarket without force? You can ask them, "Do you want to go to the supermarket?" They say no. What do you do next? You might go the easy route and bribe them, like "Let's go to the supermarket and I'll buy you a lollipop." But we all know from a lot of research and parenting experts that bribing is not the long-term solution. You could try giving choices. But how?

Choices don't always work. They must be strategically designed to get your child to willfully do what you must do at a specific point in time. What I did with my two-year-old toddler, which often worked beautifully, was: First, I stated what we were going to do; then, I gave him two choices that were not of bribing nature. These choices must be tailored to each specific child and aim to get their attention to something else, preferably something that can only be done at the supermarket (in this case). Here is what I would say to my son: "We are going to the supermarket now to buy some eggs and potatoes. When we get there, do you want to sit in the shopping cart, or do you want to walk?" As simple as this sounds, it instantly gets him thinking about the activity of sitting in a shopping cart or walking around the supermarket. Eighty percent of the time, he would stop what he was doing, and we would go. But I will even further elevate the excitement of going to the supermarket by asking him to clean up before we go. So I portrayed this activity of going to the supermarket as a reward for cleaning up toys. I would say, "Wait a second! We need to clean up the toys before we can go. Mummy is going to clean up now. Do you want to help mummy?" Then I start to slowly put some toys in the basket or in the place where they belong. Children are inherently helpful when they are in a good mood. Or, I could say, "Let's see who can clean up toys faster", making it feel like an exciting competition. Most of the time, my son will eventually, maybe instantly, help me clean up toys.

The last thing which I want to reiterate, as I have mentioned in the previous parts of the book, is to *say yes more and say no less.* What do I mean? Obviously, in life, there will be plenty of situations where you must say no. Maybe it's answering a question, maybe it's something that is plainly wrong, and you have to say, "no, it's wrong." Maybe your child is asking permission to do something, and you cannot allow it. There are plenty of situations where you simply have to say "no" to keep your life balanced, and that's fine. What I mean is, rephrase your speech to be more positive than negative. Let's imagine your child, who is in the sensitive period for language development, sees a swing, a seesaw, a sandpit, and a slide at a playground. You point at the swing and ask your child, "What is that?" Your child thinks for a minute, then points merrily at the seesaw and says "seesaw!!". What do you do in this situation? Do you keep pointing at the swing and say "no, this is a swing"? Perhaps it would be better if you redirect your own attention, point at the seesaw, and say "yes, that's a seesaw"; then point back at the swing and say, "and this is a swing"? By saying *yes* more and saying *no* less, you still achieve your goal of teaching your child the word for "a swing" but you don't discredit what they tell you (about the "seesaw"). Such seemingly small acts have a paramount impact on your child's development of not just language but also confidence, mindset, and attitude.

Non-Negotiable Boundaries
In Parenthood

There are certain boundaries and limits that are the underlying groundwork of parenting which we must respect – be it multilingual or other. These are *non-negotiable* because they affect our children's dignity and their self-perception. These boundaries might relatively shift depending on the parents, family dynamics, family structure, among other things, but generally things that must be respected in children or adults of any age come down to: *bodily autonomy, privacy/ownership,* and *personal space*. In my eyes, personal preferences also belong to the non-negotiable category, but some parents have different opinions, and they think that maybe personal preferences can be manipulated to better fit with what they want their family life to look like. However, I think that I would like to choose my battles and prefer not to fight about my son's preferences in clothing, food choices, or the color of something. These things are not critically important, at least not to me. As long as I give my son age appropriate and weather appropriate choices, I am okay with whatever choice he makes. Small leniency from my part will give my son an incredible sense of control, being respected, being heard, which in turn increases the level of trust that he has in me. That seems like a pretty good bargain to me.

The provision of these choices (or "personal preferences") must be done in a skillful way because you want your child to clearly see what their choices are. It would be very hard to deal with if you allowed your child to whine all day about wanting to wear a bathing suit to school. If you simply narrate your actions and say that "Today is nice and sunny. It would be such a good idea to wear a T-shirt with either Mickey Mouse or a dinosaur on it. Which one would you like to wear?" Once they've made their choice of T-shirt, you can continue with the choice of shorts by saying "that would go really well with the green shorts or the blue shorts, which one do you like?". Not only does this technique make the whole morning routine much more fun and positive, but it also makes your son feel like he's in control. He's made the decisions himself, which will make him feel very good about himself and about what he's wearing all day long. On the contrary, if every dressing session is a struggle, then it will keep being a struggle until he can do something that is completely out of the norm to satisfy his need for control. We don't want that, do we?

Back to *bodily autonomy* – the first "non-negotiable boundary". This essentially means that their body is their body. It's their right. Nobody should hurt them, touch them, or make physical contact with them if they don't want it. This rule does not exclude the parents. When babies are still very young, adults kiss babies all the time. And yes, babies are so cute and kissable that you just want to smoosh them all day long. But if it makes them uncomfortable and they fuss, turn away, or maybe cry while you kiss them, you should stop. I'm not even referring to hygiene and viruses, which can be transmitted from adults to babies and can be quite dangerous as babies' immune system is are significantly weaker than that of adults. I'm only talking about children's right to their own bodies. If you don't respect their bodily autonomy, you might end up with a child who becomes a bully or gets bullied at school.

Respecting your child's bodily autonomy helps them build self-respect towards their own body. It helps them love and own their body, which essentially becomes their self-confidence and self-esteem. Respected children will respect others around them. Most toddlers around eighteen to twenty-four months of age go through a phase of hitting mum, dad, and other children because they don't yet understand the concept and consequences of hurting other people. What you need to emphasize is that it is your body and you said no, so they should stop, not only because they are hurting you, but more importantly because they are invading your bodily rights.

The second "non-negotiable boundary" is *ownership*, or rather allowing your child *the right to give permission.* You should not mistake this with permissive parenting. This is respecting your child as an individual. If something belongs to your child, then you have to ask for permission to use it. This particularly applies at a playground or in playgroups, where children share toys. Children often want to play with toys that do not belong to them. If a particular toy belongs to your child, then you need to ensure that permission is sought from them. If your child doesn't agree to allow other children to play with a certain toy, then be it, that's the way it must be. The other child might cry, but your child's sense of ownership is maintained. The same applies to the opposite situation where your child goes to someone's house and they want to take something home, such as a toy that they really like. This is not permissible. You need to minimize the number of times that your child is allowed to take things from someone else's house and bring those things home. Once or twice might be OK with the owner's permission, but if it happens too often, then your child will get used to the habit of taking things from places, and it will be very difficult for you to cultivate your child's respect for value and ownership later on.

Have you ever been in a situation where your child and another child play together, each having their own toy or perhaps something bigger like bikes? Children being children, they might suddenly want to use each other's toys. While swapping is perfectly fine, as soon as the swap is completed, they realize that the other child is playing with their toy, and they start crying because they want it back. At the same time, they still want to use the other child's toy. I have been in this situation more times than necessary because we have a neighbor who has a son about my son's age. One minute they play together, the next minute they fight over something silly. Before jumping in to resolve the situation, I usually try to let them resolve it among themselves for a brief moment. If the situation escalates, then I step in but generally it is good practice to allow children some time and space to try solving the situation between themselves. In most cases, the quarrel is forgotten in a matter of minutes. If the disagreement leads to hitting and yelling, then parents need to step in. The overarching principle should be that the toys go back to their rightful owners, and if they cannot share, then they are only allowed to play with their own toy – end of story.

The third "non-negotiable boundary" is *personal space,* which essentially means ensuring your child's independence, within safety limits. When I say this, I think of the many struggles that toddlers give us in daily situations. Toddlers are little, small human beings with big personalities, big emotions, and illogical stubbornness. They often resist because they feel that they are not allowed to do things that they wish to do. Some things can be dangerous, and children should not be allowed to try them. For example, using a knife or jumping from a height are non-negotiable because our first and foremost role in parenting is to keep our children safe. As long as something is reasonably safe, then after thinking twice about it, you can consider, "Why not?". If your child wants to hold a bag of groceries for you, even though you know that it's too heavy for them, why not let them try? They will do it for maybe a second, and then they'll give it back to you because they will say it's too heavy. That one second of delay, in my opinion, is worth it to avoid a thirty-minute tantrum.

Let's say you are tidying the house when your toddler sees you sweeping the floor. They run towards you and ask you if they can do the chore for you. You know they won't be able to do the job properly, and instead of cleaning the mess, they are likely to make it messier. Ask yourself again: why not? The delay might be five minutes or ten minutes at most, but you will avoid a thirty-minute tantrum and a cranky toddler for the rest of the day. If you don't make it a battle, they will brush around and toss the dust in the air for a few minutes, then they'll get bored and continue playing elsewhere. That might take ten minutes at most. In those ten minutes, you might stand there just looking at them or taking some pictures of them sweeping the house. You could also do some other chore instead, like pick up clutter or start the laundry. Your child will get a sense of helping you, which, by the way, is a great habit to form. Even though their help is not quite effective yet, with time it will be. They will be great helpers in a few years to come. For now, instead of focusing on the effectiveness of their help, look at the mindfulness, perceptiveness, and attitude towards sharing a home with the family that your child is developing.

Another example could be daily teeth-brushing. Your toddler's teeth need to be brushed at least twice a day in the morning and in the evening before bed. In your mind, brushing your teeth must result in clean teeth, right? Yes, that's logic. But in your toddler's mind, that's not the end result, which is to *have fun*. If they don't find it fun anymore, then they start resisting. We all know it is very important to keep oral hygiene for your children. However, you need to cut yourself some slack. Imagine one day, your child is very cranky after a restless night, you're late for work, the morning routine becomes chaotic, and to top it off, your child resists brushing their teeth. The way I deal with situations like that is I just put some toothpaste on a toothbrush. I give the toothbrush to my child. Then I prepare my own toothbrush and start brushing my own teeth. I tell my son, "Brush your teeth, please". He might do it properly, merely touching his lips with the toothpaste, or he might stand motionless and give me back the toothbrush. And that's okay. Don't make a big deal out of it because the more you force him, the bigger the struggle will become overtime. He will associate brushing his teeth with something not enjoyable. Some toddlers have very big personalities, and if you miss out on three days in a row where he barely touches his teeth with a toothbrush, you might want to compensate for that missed morning with a noon or afternoon teeth-brushing session. You might try to keep your child's dental hygiene at bay by wiping their teeth with a cloth when they are being particularly difficult. Whatever you do, keep in mind that your toddler's goal for doing anything and everything is to have fun (something you and me could benefit from learning). As Maria Montessori famously said, "play is the work of a child". If something suddenly becomes not fun, that's where the struggle begins. Regardless of whether you follow science or motherly intuition (or both) when raising your children multilingually, never lose sight of all the fun and enjoyment in the process.

REFERENCES

~ numbered in order of appearance ~

[1]Kolata, G., 1984. Studying learning in the womb: Behavioral scientists are using established experimental methods to show that fetuses can and do learn. Science, 225(4659), pp.302-303.

[2]Bhamani, S., 2017. Educating before birth via talking to the baby in the womb: Prenatal innovations. Journal of Education and Educational Development, 4(2).

[3]Conboy, B.T. and Thal, D.J., 2006. Ties between the lexicon and grammar: Cross-sectional and longitudinal studies of bilingual toddlers. Child development, 77(3), pp.712-735.

[4]Parra, M., Hoff, E. and Core, C., 2011. Relations among language exposure, phonological memory, and language development in Spanish–English bilingually developing 2-year-olds. Journal of experimental child psychology, 108(1), pp.113-125.

[5]Hoff, E., Core, C., Place, S., Rumiche, R., Señor, M. and Parra, M., 2012. Dual language exposure and early bilingual development. Journal of child language, 39(1), pp.1-27.

[6]Hoff, E., Core, C., Rumiche, R. and Señor, M., 2013. Total and conceptual vocabulary in Spanish–English bilinguals from 22 to 30 months: Implications for assessment.

[7]Place, S. and Hoff, E., 2011. Properties of dual language exposure that influence 2-year-olds' bilingual proficiency. Child development, 82(6), pp.1834-1849.

[8]Ramírez-Esparza, Garcia-Sierra, A., N. and Kuhl, P.K., 2016. Relationships between quantity of language input and brain responses in bilingual and monolingual infants. International Journal of Psychophysiology, 110, pp.1-17.

[9]Conboy, B.T. and Mills, D.L., 2006. Two languages, one developing brain: Event-related potentials to words in bilingual toddlers. Developmental science, 9(1), pp.F1-F12.

[10]Genesee, F., 1989. Early bilingual development: One language or two?. Journal of child language, 16(1), pp.161-179.

[11]Heredia, R.R. and Altarriba, J., 2001. Bilingual language mixing: Why do bilinguals code-switch?. Current Directions in Psychological Science, 10(5), pp.164-168.

[12]Heredia, R.R. and Altarriba, J. eds., 2014. Foundations of bilingual memory (pp. 11-39). New York, NY, USA:: Springer.

[13]Javor, R., 2016. Bilingualism, theory of mind and perspective-taking: The effect of early bilingual exposure. Psychology and Behavioral Sciences, 5(6), pp.143-148.

[14]Crinion, J., Turner, R., Grogan, A., Hanakawa, T., Noppeney, U., Devlin, J.T., Aso, T., Urayama, S., Fukuyama, H., Stockton, K. and Usui, K., 2006. Language control in the bilingual brain. Science, 312(5779), pp.1537-1540.

[15]Luk, G., Green, D.W., Abutalebi, J. and Grady, C., 2012. Cognitive control for language switching in bilinguals: A quantitative meta-analysis of functional neuroimaging studies. Language and cognitive processes, 27(10), pp.1479-1488.

[16]Steele, J.L., Slater, R.O., Zamarro, G., Miller, T., Li, J., Burkhauser, S. and Bacon, M., 2017. Effects of dual-language immersion programs on student achievement: Evidence from lottery data. American Educational Research Journal, 54(1_suppl), pp.282S-306S.

[17]Thomas, W.P. and Collier, V., 1997. School Effectiveness for Language Minority Students. NCBE Resource Collection Series, No. 9.

[18]Martin-Rhee, M.M. and Bialystok, E., 2008. The development of two types of inhibitory control in monolingual and bilingual children. Bilingualism: language and cognition, 11(1), pp.81-93.

[19]Luna, D., Ringberg, T. and Peracchio, L.A., 2008. One individual, two identities: Frame switching among biculturals. Journal of consumer research, 35(2), pp.279-293.

[20]Pearson, B.Z., 1998. Assessing lexical development in bilingual babies and toddlers. International journal of bilingualism, 2(3), pp.347-372.

[21]Pearson, B.Z. and Fernández, S.C., 1994. Patterns of interaction in the lexical growth in two languages of bilingual infants and toddlers. Language learning, 44(4), pp.617-653.

[22]Krashen, S.D., 1973. Lateralization, language learning, and the critical period: Some new evidence. Language learning, 23(1), pp.63-74.

[23]Senechal, M. and Cornell, E.H., 1993. Vocabulary acquisition through shared reading experiences. Reading research quarterly, pp.360-374.

[24]Robbins, C. and Ehri, L.C., 1994. Reading storybooks to kindergartners helps them learn new vocabulary words. Journal of Educational psychology, 86(1), p.54.

[25]Kadesjö, C., Kadesjö, B., Hägglöf, B. and Gillberg, C., 2001. ADHD in Swedish 3-to 7-year-old children. Journal of the American Academy of Child & Adolescent Psychiatry, 40(9), pp.1021-1028.

[26]Lin, Y.-C., Li, K.-H., Sung, W.-S., Ko, H.-W., Tzeng, O. J. L., Hung, D. L., & Juan, C.-H. (2011). The relationship between development of attention and learning in children A cognitive neuroscience approach. Bulletin of Educational Psychology, 42(3), 517–542.

[27]Renninger, K.A., 1992. Individual interest and development: Implications for theory and practice. The role of interest in learning and development, 26(3-4), pp.361-395. [book chapter]

[28]Flavell, J.H., 1963. The developmental psychology of Jean Piaget. D Van Nostrand.

[29]Richardson, A.C., Lo, J., Priddis, L. and O'Sullivan, T.A., 2020. A quasi-experimental study of the respectful approach on early parenting competence and stress. Journal of child and family studies, 29, pp.2796-2810.

Books that informed my general research:

Arnberg, L., 1987. *Raising Children Bilingually: The Pre-School Years. Multilingual Matters 27*. Multilingual Matters Ltd.., Bank House, 8a Hill Road, Clevedon, Avon BS21 7HH, England, United Kingdom (ISBN-0-905028-70-8, paperback: 6.95 British pounds, US $15; ISBN-0-9050281-71-6, hardback)..

Cantone, K.F., 2007. *Code-switching in bilingual children* (Vol. 296). Dordrecht: Springer.

King, K.A. and Mackey, A., 2007. *The bilingual edge: Why, when, and how to teach your child a second language*. New York: Collins.

Raguenaud, V., 2010. *Bilingual by choice: Raising kids in two (or more!) languages*. Nicholas Brealey. (B

Steiner, N., Hayes, S. and Parker, S., 2008. *7 steps to raising a bilingual child*. Amacom.

Tokuhama-Espinosa, T., 2001. *Raising Multilingual Children: Foreign Language Acquisition and Children*. Bergin and Garvey.

ABOUT THE AUTHOR

I am first and foremost a mother. As a day job, I am a university lecturer. I have a PhD in Education from RMIT University in Vietnam, a Master's degree in International Accounting from Royal Holloway University of London in the UK, and a Bachelor's degree in Finance and Accounting from Kozminski University in Poland.

I speak three languages:
English, Vietnamese, and Polish.

These three languages are used on a regular basis in my daily life, especially English and Vietnamese, which I use for work and hobbies such as reading. I use Polish to read books and converse with my Polish friends. I also learned Spanish for a few years, but lost fluency because I didn't use it often enough. Though I can understand Spanish here and there, I'm not confident enough to say I can command it well. I hope to learn at least one or two more languages in this lifetime, maybe together with my son.

Having grown up in a multilingual environment and hence gaining proficiency in three languages quite effortlessly, helped me recognize and appreciate the importance of knowing and commanding multiple languages. I have worked in Poland, England, as well as Vietnam, and nowhere did I feel challenged in terms of languages. I am admittedly not very familiar with the sensation of being left out due to not understanding a conversation; it is rather down to other factors as to whether I can or want to participate. While merely understanding what is being said around you is not enough to get through life, it is definitely a very valuable key to hold in your hand and open multiple doors beyond borders.

My parents are both monolingual, but my brother and I grew up trilingual. We both started our education in Poland at Polish-speaking schools, but as soon as we got home, we had to switch to Vietnamese. We didn't like it as it was the minority language for us, we found it easier and more natural to communicate in the majority language (Polish). Polish was almost like our secret sibling language at home because my parents were not particularly fluent in it. But my parents were extremely persistent, especially my dad, who made it his life's mission to be a patrolman in our lives and made sure we only spoke Vietnamese to each other at home (or at least in his earshot).

I think it is an invaluable gift that our parents have given us, thanks to which we now tend to feel we have been dealt an upper hand in life - three languages just like that, for free, with almost no conscious effort. Don't get me wrong; my life is not all smooth sailing. Some might even say I have had it rough. But to me, it has been an adventure, and I welcome many more.

THE END